图解初级英语语法

王全民　编著

江苏凤凰科学技术出版社·南京

图书在版编目（CIP）数据

图解初级英语语法 / 王全民编著. — 南京 : 江苏
凤凰科学技术出版社, 2023.5
ISBN 978-7-5713-3248-8

Ⅰ. ①图… Ⅱ. ①王… Ⅲ. ①英语—语法—自学参考
资料 Ⅳ. ①H314

中国版本图书馆CIP数据核字(2022)第191815号

图解初级英语语法

编　　　　著	王全民	
责 任 编 辑	陈　艺	
责 任 校 对	仲　敏	
责 任 监 制	方　晨	

出 版 发 行	江苏凤凰科学技术出版社	
出版社地址	南京市湖南路 1 号 A 楼，邮编：210009	
出版社网址	http://www.pspress.cn	
印　　　　刷	河南瑞之光印刷股份有限公司	

开　　　　本	718 mm × 1 000 mm　1/16	
印　　　　张	18	
字　　　　数	238 000	
版　　　　次	2023年5月第1版	
印　　　　次	2023年5月第1次印刷	

标 准 书 号	ISBN 978-7-5713-3248-8
定　　　　价	68.00元

图书如有印装质量问题，可随时向我社印务部调换。

目录
CONTENTS

第四章 数量词 Quantifiers

第五章 介词 Prepositions

第六章 形容词和副词 Adjectives and Adverbs

第七章 连词 Conjunctions

第八章 动词 Verbs

第九章　基本句式 Basic Sentences

第十章　简单句 Simple Sentences

第十一章　主谓一致 Subject-predicate Consistency

第十二章 一般时 Simple Tense

第十三章 将来时 Future Tense

第十四章 进行时 Continuous Tense

第十五章 完成时 Perfect Tense

第十六章 被动语态 Passive Voice

第一章

冠词
Articles

第一单元 不定冠词 a, an 的用法

1 不定冠词 a 和 an 都用在可数名词的单数形式前。an 用在元音音素开头的单数可数名词前，a 用在辅音音素开头的单数可数名词前。

a boy 一个男孩　　　　a cat 一只猫

an egg 一个鸡蛋　　　an umbrella 一把伞

元音字母一共有五个：a, e, i, o, u, 但并非所有以元音字母开头的单词都是在其前加不定冠词 an。比如 uniform, 虽以元音字母 u 开头，但是其第一个发音是 [j]，所以表示"一件制服"时，不能用 an uniform，要用 a uniform。还有一些名词虽不是元音字母开头，但是第一个音是元音，其前面的不定冠词用 an，如 an hour（一小时）。

2 a/an 可表示人或物区别于其他物种。

- A horse is not as strong as a lion.
  马没有狮子那么强壮。
  （这里的 A horse 和 a lion 指一个物种。）
- Mr. Smith is an English.
  史密斯先生是英国人。
  （这里的 an 用于表示某一类人。）

3 a/an 表示数量"一"。

- I have a book.
  我有一本书。
- She gave me an orange.
  她给了我一个橘子。

4 a/an 可以用在有形容词修饰的名词前。

- He is an honest boy.
  他是一个诚实的男孩。
- She wears a green sweater.
  她穿着一件绿色的毛衣。

5 a/an 可以表示"每"。

- We meet each other once a week.
  我们每周见一次面。
- The car runs 70 kilometers an hour.
  这辆车时速 70 千米。

6 a/an 可以用在一些固定搭配中。

in a minute 立刻，马上　　a lot of 许多

in a hurry 急忙，匆忙　　quite a 相当

a piece of ... 一片……

after a while 一会儿

have a cold/fever/break 感冒 / 发热 / 休息

Exercise

一、结合图片，在下面空格处填上不定冠词 **a** 或者 **an**。

1. _____ beautiful girl

2. _____ hour late

3. _____ weak tiger

4. _____ butterfly

5. _____ onion

6. _____ university

二、选出正确的答案。

1. I want ○ an ○ a doll as my birthday present（礼物）.

2. ○ An ○ A pear is ○ an ○ a kind of fruit.

3. My sister has ○ an ○ a orange coat.

4. I bought ○ an ○ a storybook.

5. My mother gave me ○ an ○ a banana and some bread.

6. We saw ○ an ○ a elephant in the zoo.

7. Do you have ○ an ○ a dictionary（字典）?

8. Bicycle（自行车）is ○ an ○ a useful tool for us.

参考答案：

一、1. a　2. an　3. a　4. a　5. an　6. a

二、1. a　2. A; a　3. an　4. a　5. a　6. an　7. a　8. a

第二单元 定冠词 the 的用法

the 的用法

表示特指的人或物
- **The** apples on **the** table got bad.

  桌子上的苹果变质了。

指前面已经提到过的人或物
- Here's a book of *Pride and Prejudice*. **The** book is very famous.

  这儿有一本《傲慢与偏见》。这本书很有名。

表示说话双方都知道的人或物
- We can't catch **the** bus.

  我们赶不上这一趟公交车了。

用在世界上独一无二的事物之前
the moon 月亮　**the** sun 太阳

用在序数词以及形容词的最高级前
the first place 第一名

the strongest animal 最强壮的动物

用在表示方位、方向的名词前
- My home is behind **the** school.

  我家在学校后面。

用在表示江河、海洋和山脉的名词前
- I want to climb **the** Mount Tai.

  我想去爬泰山。

用在表示乐器的名词前
- Lily can play **the** piano.

  莉莉会弹钢琴。

用在由两个或以上的普通名词构成的专有名词前
- **The** Great Wall lies in China.

  长城位于中国。

用在姓氏的复数形式前，表示一家人
the Greens 格林一家

the Whites 怀特一家

用于构成固定搭配
in **the** end 最后

at **the** same time 与此同时

by **the** way 顺便说一下

on **the** whole 总的来说

用在表示身体部位的名词前
- He was wounded in **the** head.

  他的头受伤了。

用在中国节日前
the Mid-autumn Festival 中秋节

the Spring Festival 春节

the 与复数连用，表示整体。如：

the teachers of the school 全体老师

teachers of the school 部分老师

Exercise

一、找出下列句子的错误之处并改正。

1. A cup on a table dropped down. _____

2. His seat is on left of that desk. _____

3. We must get up earlier to catch a early bus. _____

4. Mr. Smith will give speech in United States. _____

5. The Green are going to have a picnic tomorrow. _____

6. I can't play a violin well. _____

7. Rich should give a hand to poor. _____

二、根据图片提示，将下面句子补充完整。

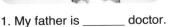

1. My father is _____ doctor.

2. Linda is playing _____ guitar.

3. _____ sun is in _____ sky.

4. I have _____ apple. _____ apple is sweet.

5. _____ Smiths all like traveling.

6. There is nobody on _____ bus.

参考答案：

一、1. 第二个 a 改为 the　2. on 后面加 the　3. a 改为 the　4. give 后面加 a，in 后面加 the
　　5. Green 改为 Greens　6. a 改为 the　7. Rich 改为 The rich，poor 前面加 the

二、1. a　2. the　3. The; the　4. an; The　5. The　6. the

第三单元 零冠词

零冠词的用法

用在表示国名、地名和人名的名词前
- John comes from Australia.

  约翰来自澳大利亚。

用在表示三餐和球类运动的名词前
- We often play basketball after dinner.

  我们经常在晚餐后打篮球。

用在表示季节、星期、月份、日期、节日等的名词前
- Tony's birthday is August 5th. It is Saturday.

  托尼的生日是八月五日，那天是周六。

用在表示职位、头衔和称呼的名词前
Uncle Mike 迈克叔叔

Dr. Wilson 威尔逊博士

用在两个或两个以上并列的不可数名词前
water and soil 水和土壤

day and night 白天黑夜

用在有指示代词 / 不定代词 / 物主代词修饰的名词前
- My home is over there.

  我家在那儿。

用在和 by 连用的表示交通工具的名词前
- I go to work by subway.

  我乘地铁上班。

除了介词 by 和交通工具连用可以不使用冠词外，其他"动词 / 介词 + 交通工具"的中间要使用冠词。如：take a taxi 乘坐出租车，on the bus 在公交车上

用在一些固定短语中
not at all 一点儿也不　　take care of 照顾

in time 及时　　　　　　after all 毕竟

Exercise

根据图片提示，从下面方框中选出对应的单词并添加合适的冠词填入空格处，每个词只能使用一次。

egg   schoolbag   winter   boy   plane   lunch
table   soccer   Johnny   Doctor Smith

1. Do you know _____ with short hair?

2. I usually travel by _____.

3. My mother often has _____ for breakfast.

4. Bill is playing _____ with his classmates.

5. My _____ is heavy.

6. My favorite season is _____.

7. We usually have_____ at 12:00.

8. _____ is under _____.

9. _____ is on duty（值班）.

参考答案：

1. the boy   2. plane   3. an egg   4. soccer   5. schoolbag

6. winter   7. lunch   8. Johnny; the table   9. Doctor Smith

第四单元 冠词的"泛指"

1 "零冠词 + 复数名词"表示一类人或事物，此时为泛指。

- Are they **teachers** or **dancers**?
  他们是老师还是舞者？
- My father and mother are both **lawyers**.
  我的爸爸和妈妈都是律师。

2 "零冠词 + 不可数名词"泛指一类。

- **Water** is important to life.
  水对生活很重要。
- We can't live without **air**.
  我们离不开空气。

3 "a/an + 可数名词单数"泛指"某个"。

- He isn't allowed to keep **a cat**.
  他不被允许养猫。
- **A man** is swimming in the pool.
  有人在泳池里游泳。

4 "the + 可数名词单数"表示一类人或物。

- She is **the girl** who likes to dress up.
  她是一个爱打扮的女孩。
- **The tomato** is a kind of vegetable.
  西红柿是一种蔬菜。

5 "the + 国家 / 民族"表示整个民族。

the Chinese 中国人
the American 美国人
the Indian 印第安人
the Islam 伊斯兰教

6 "the + 形容词"表示某一类人。

the old 老年人　　the young 年轻人
the rich 富人　　　the poor 穷人
the blind 盲人　　the wounded 伤员

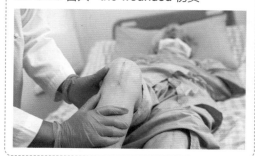

Exercise

一、根据图片提示将下列冠词和名词匹配，并填写在空格处。

| a   an   the   / | | English   cup   workers   pear
girl   professor White |

1. _____ is for drinking water.

2. _____ is an expert in chemistry.

3. _____ likes shopping.

4. Alice is _____ teacher.

5. _____ are tired.

6. This is _____.

二、将下面单词按正确的顺序排列成句子，并翻译。

1. is a animal tiger a dangerous _____

2. is there on umbrella the table an _____

3. leaf a tree from the falls _____

4. working are hard workers _____

参考答案：

一、1. A cup   2. Professor White   3. The girl   4. an English   5. Workers   6. a pear

二、1. A tiger is a dangerous animal. 老虎是一种危险的动物。

　　2. There is an umbrella on the table. 桌子上有一把伞。

　　3. A leaf falls from the tree. 树叶从树上落下。

　　4. Workers are working hard. 工人们在努力工作。

第五单元 同一词组使用不同冠词时的意义

{ in front of ... 在……（外部）的前面
{ in the front of ... 在……（内部）的前面

- Bob is standing **in front of** the building.
  鲍勃正站在建筑前面。
- Mike stands **in the front of** the classroom.
  迈克站在教室的前面。

{ in the hospital 在医院（不一定是生病
{ 住院，有可能是探望病人或在医院工作）
{ in hospital 生病住院

- Sarah works **in the hospital**.
  萨拉在医院里工作。
- Nick was **in hospital** two days ago.
  尼克两天前住院了。

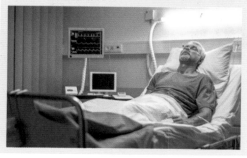

{ go to the church 去教堂（不一定是去
{ 做礼拜）
{ go to church 去教堂做礼拜

◎ 这样的词还有 class，school，college，
market，bed 等。

- I went to **the church** yesterday.
  我昨天去了教堂。
- My grandma **goes to church** on Sunday.
  我奶奶周日去教堂做礼拜。

{ at the table 在桌子旁（不一定是在吃饭）
{ at table 在吃饭

- The kids sit **at the table** one by one.
  孩子们一个挨一个地坐在桌子旁边。
- My little brother is **at table**.
  我的弟弟在吃饭。

{ in future（从今以后的）将来
{ in the future（较为遥远的）将来

- I'll study hard **in future**.
  从今以后我会努力学习。
- I want to be an engineer **in the future**.
  我将来想成为一名工程师。

{ on earth 究竟
{ on the earth 在地球上，在地上

- What **on earth** did you do?
  你究竟做了什么？
- A white cat is lying **on the earth**.
  一只白色的猫正躺在地上。

一、找出下列句子的错误之处并改正，并为其匹配正确的图片。

1. She is writing at a table.

2. It's time to go to the bed.

3. He goes to a bed to take care of the baby.

4. I often go to school on the foot.

5. Emily went to a hospital.

二、请为下面的句子勾选出正确的冠词。

1. ○ The ○ / Washington is the capital of America.

2. Lincoln was ○ the ○ a great president of America.

3. We usually have ○ / ○ a dinner at 6:00 p.m.

4. Failure is ○ the ○ / mother of success.

5. Kate is going to play ○ the ○ / volleyball with her friends.

6. We all think of ○ the ○ / British as gentlemen.

7. Alice goes to ○ the ○ / hospital. Because her mother is in ○ / ○ the hospital.

8. Farmers have ○ the ○ a rest under the tree.

9. This is ○ the ○ a university I'm going to study in ○ / ○ the future.

10. Lucy loves eating ○ / ○ an orange every morning.

参考答案：
一、1. a 改为 the   2. 去掉 the   3. a 改为 the   4. 去掉 the   5. 去掉 a
　　1—b　2—c　3—d　4—a　5—e
二、1. /　2. a　3. /　4. the　5. /　6. the　7. the; /　8. a　9. the; the　10. an

第二章

名词
Nouns

第一单元 专有名词

- 人名
- 朝代、星期、月份、节日等表示时间的词
- 洲、国家、城市等地名
- 建筑名、街道名
- 团体机构名、组织名
- 特有的景点
- 书名、电影名

1. 专有名词的首字母要大写。
2. 通常，专有名词前不加冠词，但表示江、河、山脉、群岛等地理名称的专有名词以及由两个以上的普通名词组成的专有名词之前要加定冠词 the。

1 人名

Professor Davis 戴维斯教授   **Cinderella** 灰姑娘

2 朝代、星期、月份、节日等表示时间的词

Sunday 周日
May 五月
Tudor Dynasty 都铎王朝
Christmas 圣诞节

3 洲、国家、城市等地名

Europe 欧洲
Italy 意大利
Venice 威尼斯

4 建筑名、街道名

White House 白宫
the Second Avenue 第二大道

5 团体机构、组织名

the United Nations 联合国   **the Red Cross** 红十字会

6 特有的景点

the Imperial Palace 故宫   **the Taj Mahal** 泰姬陵

7 书名、电影名

- My father bought *Harry Potter* for me.
  我爸爸给我买了《哈利·波特》。
- *Titanic* is one of my favorite movies.
  《泰坦尼克号》是我最喜欢的电影之一。

 **Exercise**

一、请从下列单词中挑选出专有名词，并写在右边的方框中。

Apple	Chair
the Great Wall	Book
United States	Asia
Alice	China
the Spring Festival	Monday
Bed	April
Beijing	Flower
World Trade Organization (WTO)	
Age	People

专有名词

二、圈出下列句子书写错误的专有名词，并改正。

1. My uncle works in america. 我的叔叔在美国工作。

2. The thanksgiving Day is coming. 感恩节来了。

3. Great Wall is one of the great wonders of the world. 长城是世界奇迹之一。

4. My family plan to have a party on sunday. 我们全家计划周日举行一个聚会。

5. Nick lives in the third avenue. 尼克居住在第三大道。

6. Spring is from March to may. 春季是从三月到五月。

7. The capital of china is Beijing. 中国的首都是北京。

参考答案：

一、the Great Wall, United States, Asia, Alice, China, the Spring Festival, Monday, April, Beijing, World Trade Organization (WTO)

二、1. america—America   2. 去掉 the，thanksgiving—Thanksgiving

3. Great Wall——The Great Wall   4. sunday—Sunday

5. the third avenue—the Third Avenue   6. may—May

7. china—China

第二单元　普通名词

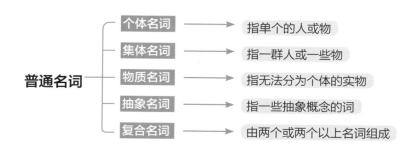

普通名词
- 个体名词 ——→ 指单个的人或物
- 集体名词 ——→ 指一群人或一些物
- 物质名词 ——→ 指无法分为个体的实物
- 抽象名词 ——→ 指一些抽象概念的词
- 复合名词 ——→ 由两个或两个以上名词组成

1 个体名词指的是单个的人或者物。

table 桌子	cup 杯子	hat 帽子
chair 椅子	bottle 瓶子	bag 包
bed 床	picture 照片	watch 手表

2 集体名词指的是某些人或物的总称。

- The **police** caught a thief.
  警察抓到了一个小偷。
- When he arrived, his **family** had already left.
  当他到达的时候，他的家人已经离开了。

3 物质名词指的是无法判断个体的事物。

- I have **bread** and **milk** for breakfast.
  我早餐吃面包和牛奶。
- My mom always drinks a glass of **wine** before going to bed.
  我妈妈总是在睡前喝一杯葡萄酒。
- This table is made of **wood**.
  这张桌子是木头做的。

4 抽象名词指的是动作、状态、情感或品质等表示抽象意义的词。

- It was a **pity** to lose this opportunity.
  失去这次机会很可惜。
- It's all my **fault**.
  这全都是我的错。
- We are proud of his **behavior**.
  我们为他的表现感到骄傲。

5 复合名词是由两个或两个以上的名词直接连在一起构成的。

news（新闻）+ **paper**（纸）= newspaper 报纸

home（家）+ **work**（工作）= homework 家庭作业

police（警察）+ **man**（男人）= policeman 男警察

Exercise

结合图片和首字母，将下面的单词补充完整，并将单词分类。

1. p_____   2. r_____   3. f_____   4. f_____   5. w_____

6. m_____   7. a_____   8. m_____   9. s_____   10. f_____

11. a_____   12. s_____   13. a_____   14. c_____   15. e_____

个体名词	集体名词	物质名词	抽象名词

参考答案：

1. people   2. rice   3. football   4. furniture   5. water   6. monkey   7. anger   8. meat
9. sadness   10. flour   11. audience   12. student   13. animal   14. computer
15. excitement

个体名词：football，monkey，student，computer

集体名词：furniture，audience，animal，people

物质名词：rice，flour，water，meat

抽象名词：anger，sadness，excitement

第三单元 可数名词

可数名词有单数与复数两种形式

可数名词单数表示数量为"一"

不定冠词 $\begin{cases} \text{a boy 一个男孩} \\ \text{a potato 一个土豆} \end{cases}$

可数名词复数表示数量为"两个或以上"

数量 $\begin{cases} \text{two boys 两个男孩} \\ \text{three potatoes 三个土豆} \end{cases}$

1 可数名词包括人、动物和有具体形状的物。

- There is **a cow** on the grass.
  草地上有一头牛。
- This **plant** grows very well.
  这株植物长得很好。

2 抽象名词一般情况下是不可数名词，但如果将其具体化的话，就会变成可数名词。

- It's a good **way** to learn math.
  这是学习数学的好方法。
- That sounds like a good **idea**.
  这听起来是个好主意。

3 当单数可数名词表示泛指时，前面要用不定冠词 a/an；当单数可数名词表示特指时，前面要用定冠词 the。

- Can you give me **an eraser**?
  你能给我一块橡皮吗？　没有特指
- Can you give me **the eraser** on the desk?
  你能把桌子上的橡皮给我吗？　特指

4 可数名词可以由量词修饰。

a number of 许多	the number of 数目
many 许多	few/a few 很少
only a few 几乎没有	quite a few 不少，相当多
not a few 不少，相当多	many a 许多的（后面跟单数可数名词）

- **A number of** students took part in that event.
  许多学生参与了那次事件。
- **Many a** store is on sale.
  许多商店都在促销。

5 可数名词单数搭配动词单数形式使用；可数名词复数搭配动词复数形式使用。

- **Those children are** playing basketball.
  那些孩子们在打篮球。
- There **are two peaches** on the table.
  桌子上有两个桃子。

6 针对可数名词的数量进行提问时要使用 how many。

- **How many** students are there in your class?
  你班上有多少学生？

选取合适的修饰词放在名词前面，并将其写在右边的图片下面。

a

an

some

beef noodles

egg

carrot

apple

hamburger

onion

tomato

strawberry

1. _____

2. _____

3. _____

4. _____

5. _____

6. _____

7. _____

8. _____

参考答案：

1. some tomatoes　2. some beef noodles　3. an egg　4. some carrots

5. some strawberries　6. an apple　7. some onions　8. a hamburger

第四单元 不可数名词

不可数名词指不能一个一个数出来，即不能用数量表示的名词。

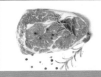
meat 肉

laughter 笑声

tea 茶

cotton 棉花

1 不可数名词不能用不定冠词 **a/an** 修饰，只能用定冠词 **the** 来修饰，在句中一般用作单数形式。

• **The beef tastes** good.
牛肉吃起来不错。

• **The water is** too hot.
水太烫了。

2 两种或两种以上不可数名词充当主语时，谓语动词用复数。 谓语用复数

• **Water and electricity play** an important role in our lives. 水、电是不可数名词
水和电在我们的生活中扮演着重要的角色。

水果、牛奶、面包是不可数名词

• **Fruit, milk and bread are** all my favorites.
水果、牛奶和面包我都爱吃。 谓语用复数

3 可数名词和不可数名词是非常灵活的。由于很多名词具有多种含义，所以同一个名词在一个场合是可数名词，在另一个场合又变成了不可数名词。

类别	可数	不可数
表示动物的名词	chicken(s) 小鸡	chicken 鸡肉
	lamb(s) 羊羔	lamb 羊羔肉
物质名词	room(s) 房间	room 空间
	glass(es) 玻璃杯	glass 玻璃
抽象名词	a success 一件（个）成功的事（人）	success 成功
	exercise(s) 练习	exercise 锻炼

4 不可数名词的复数形式用数词和量词来表示。

• I often have **a glass of water** after getting up.
我经常起床后喝一杯水。

一些不可数名词在固定短语中可用作可数名词
take a **walk** 散步
catch a **cold** 感冒
take a **break** 休息
make a **living** 谋生

• I want **two cups of coffee.**
我想要两杯咖啡。

5 用 **how much** 来提问不可数名词。

• **How much soup** do you want?
你想要多少汤？

有一些词可以用来修饰不可数名词：
much 许多；little/a little 很少
a great deal of 大量的
a large amount of/large amounts of 大量的
还有一些词既可以修饰可数名词又可以修饰不可数名词：
some 一些；any 任何
a lot of/lots of 很多
plenty of 很多

Exercise

一、圈出下列句子中的不可数名词。

1. He drank so much milk. 他喝了很多牛奶。

2. For me, a piece of bread is enough. 对我来说，一片面包足够了。

3. There is some water on the floor. 地上有一些水。

4. Would you like to give me some advice? 你愿意给我一些建议吗？

5. The chicken is delicious. 鸡肉很美味。

6. My dad knows many kinds of fishes, because he likes fish. 我爸爸知道很多鱼类，因为他喜欢吃鱼肉。

7. We were surprised by the news. 我们对这个消息感到惊讶。

8. The classroom was filled with laughter. 教室里充满了笑声。

二、根据图片和汉语意思的提示，从方框中选出合适的词填在空格处。

> **much   cups   some   glass   a**

Waitress: Excuse me. May I have your order? 打扰一下，现在点餐吗？

Carl: I want two _____ of coffee. 我要两杯咖啡。

Carl: What do you want? 你想要什么？

Bill: I'm hungry, so I'd like to eat _____ beef and rice. 我很饿，所以我想要一些牛肉和米饭。

Waitress: Sorry, the beef has been sold out. 抱歉，牛肉已经卖完了。

Bill: Alright. Give me _____ chicken with _____ salt. 好吧。给我一些鸡肉，多点儿盐。

Waitress: Okay. Drinks? 好的，喝的呢？

Bill: A _____ of wine. 一杯葡萄酒。

Waitress: Anything else? 还要其他的吗？

Alice: I want _____ salad. 给我来一份沙拉。

Waitress: No problem. Just a minute. 没问题，请稍等。

参考答案：

一、1. milk   2. bread   3. water   4. advice   5. chicken   6. fish   7. news   8. laughter

二、cups，some，some，much，glass，a

21

第五单元 名词复数的规则变化

名词的单数形式用来表示某"一个"物体，名词的复数形式用来表示"两个或两个以上"的某物。名词复数的变化分为规则变化和不规则变化，规则变化要遵循一定的规律。

1 通常直接加 -s，同时该单词的读音发生变化，清辅音后读 /s/，浊辅音和元音后读 /z/。

book → book + s = books /bʊks/ 书

orange → orange + s = oranges /'ɔrɪndʒz/ 橘子

2 以 -s，-x，-sh，-ch 结尾的单词，在词尾加 -es，发音 /ɪz/。

bus → bus + es = buses /'bʌsɪz/ 公交车

box → box + es = boxes /baksɪz/ 盒子

brush → brush + es = brushes /brʌʃɪz/ 刷子

watch → watch + es = watches /wɒtʃɪz/ 手表

3 以"辅音字母 +y"结尾的单词，将 y 变 i，再加 -es，发音 /ɪz/。

baby → babi + es = babies /'bebɪz/ 婴儿

city → citi + es = cities /'sɪtɪz/ 城市

4 以"元音字母 +y"结尾的单词，直接加 -s，发音 /z/。

boy → boy + s = boys /bɔɪz/ 男孩

toy → toy + s = toys /tɔɪz/ 玩具

5 以 -o 结尾的单词，有生命的加 -es，无生命的加 -s，发音 /z/。

tomato → tomato + es = tomatoes /tə'metoz/
西红柿 有生命

photo → photo + s = photos /'fotoz/ 照片
无生命

6 以 -f 或 -fe 结尾的单词，将 -f 或 -fe 变为 -v，再加 -es，发音 /vz/。

leaf → leav + es = leaves /livz/ 树叶

wife → wiv + es = wives /waɪvz/ 妻子

★有些以 -f 或 -fe 结尾的名词可以直接加 -s。

roof → roof + s = roofs 房顶

★还有一些以 f 结尾的名词，既可以直接加 -s，也可以将 f 变为 v，再加 -es。

hoof → hoofs/hooves 马蹄

scarf → scarfs/scarves 围巾

一、写出下列名词的复数形式。

1. watermelon 西瓜

_____

2. banana 香蕉

_____

3. peach 桃子

_____

4. apple 苹果

_____

5. mango 芒果

_____

6. tomato 西红柿

_____

7. orange 橘子

_____

8. pepper 辣椒

_____

9. grape 葡萄

_____

10. eggplant 茄子

_____

11. carrot 胡萝卜

_____

12. pomegranate 石榴

_____

13. pineapple 菠萝

_____

14. pumpkin 南瓜

_____

15. celery 芹菜

_____

二、找出下列句子的错误之处并改正。

1. I kept three cat. _____

2. We took a lot of photoes at the zoo. _____

3. He made friends with two Frenchmans in France. _____

4. Many peoples wear scarfes on the street. _____

5. All the toies fell down from the cupboard. _____

参考答案:

一、1. watermelons 2. bananas 3. peaches 4. apples 5. mangos/mangoes
6. tomatoes 7. oranges 8. peppers 9. grapes 10. eggplants 11. carrots
12. pomegranates 13. pineapples 14. pumpkins 15. celeries

二、1. cat → cats 2. photoes → photos 3. Frenchmans → Frenchmen
4. peoples → people 5. toies → toys

第六单元 名词复数的不规则变化

1 改变元音字母

man → men 男人　　foot → feet 脚

mouse → mice 老鼠　　tooth → teeth 牙齿

★如果是由 man 或者 woman 组成的复合词，则需要将复合词都变为复数形式。

man doctor → men doctors 男医生（们）

woman teacher → women teachers 女教师（们）

★当复合词的形式为"其他词 + man/woman"时，其复数形式只把 man/woman 变为 men/women。

policeman → policemen 男警察（们）

policewoman → policewomen 女警察（们）

2 在词尾加 -en 或 -ren

ox → ox + en = oxen 公牛

child → child + ren = children 孩子

3 复合名词的复数形式是把主要词变为复数形式

on-looker → on-lookers 旁观者

mother-in-law → mothers-in-law 岳母

4 有的单词单复数同形

deer → deer 鹿

sheep → sheep 羊

means → means 方法

fish 是一个比较特殊的名词，当表示"鱼"时，是单复同形的可数名词。当 fish 表示"鱼肉"时，是不可数名词；表示"鱼的种类"时，是可数名词，其复数形式是 fishes。

5 某国人的复数形式

◎ 以 ese 结尾的"某国人"单复数同形

Chinese → Chinese 中国人

Japanese → Japanese 日本人

◎ 把 man 变为 men

Englishman → Englishmen 英国人

Frenchman → Frenchmen 法国人

◎ 在后面直接加 -s

German → German + s = Germans 德国人

American → American + s = Americans 美国人

表达具体的数目时，前面要加量词：

a pair of glasses 一副眼镜

two pairs of shoes 两双鞋

6 可数名词单、复数形式的特殊意义

意义	示例
一些集体名词形式上是单数，但通常用作复数意义	police 警察　cattle 牲畜
一些集体名词指整体时，用单数形式；指集体中的个体时，用复数形式	family 家庭　army 军队
一些名词以 -s 结尾，但用作单数形式	the United Nations 联合国　physics 物理
一些抽象名词虽为复数形式，但表示具体的事物	joys 令人高兴的事　failures 失败的事情
一些由两部分组成的物品，只有复数形式	glasses 眼镜　jeans 牛仔裤　shoes 鞋子

 **Exercise**

一、根据句意，将括号中名词的正确形式填在空格处。

1. _____ (mouse) always steal food at night. 老鼠总是在晚上偷吃粮食。

2. I brush my _____ (tooth) every night. 我每天晚上都刷牙。

3. My mother goes to work on _____ (feet) . 我妈妈走路上班。

4. Where are my _____ (glass) ? 我的眼镜在哪儿?

5. Peter can't find his _____ (shoe) . 皮特找不到他的鞋了。

6. _____ (physics) is one of my favorite subjects. 物理是我最喜欢的学科之一。

7. _____ (sheep) are not as strong as cattle. 羊不像牛那么强壮。

8. The _____ (woman teacher) are more than _____ (man teacher) in our school. 我们学校里的女老师比男老师多。

9. There are some _____（child) flying kites in the park. 有一些孩子在公园里放风筝。

10. Chinese _____（people) are used to eating with chopsticks. 中国人习惯用筷子吃饭。

二、为下列句子勾选正确的答案。

1. I want ○ a ○ a pair of new gloves for Christmas. 我圣诞节想要一双新手套。

2. These new shoes ○ are ○ is a little small for me. 这双新鞋对我来说有点小。

3. Maybe you need two pairs of ○ sunglasses ○ sunglass. 或许你需要两副太阳镜。

4. Police ○ is ○ are on duty. 警察正在值班。

5. The engine ○ failure ○ failures makes Mike disappointed. 发动机故障使迈克感到很失望。

6. We prepared potatoes and ○ fishes ○ fish for supper. 我们的晚餐准备了土豆和鱼肉。

参考答案:
一、1. Mice   2. teeth   3. foot   4. glasses   5. shoes   6. Physics
　　7. Sheep   8. women teachers; men teachers   9. children   10. people
二、1. a pair of   2. are   3. sunglasses   4. are   5. failure   6. fish

第七单元 名词的 's 所有格

名词所有格是用来表示名词之间的所属关系，相当于汉语中的"……的"。's 所有格表示含有生命特征的名词的所属关系。

结构

1 单数名词加 's → 名词所有格

Lily's book 莉莉的书

mother's bag 妈妈的包

2 以 s/es 结尾的复数名词加 ' → 名词所有格

teachers' pens 老师们的笔

parents' presents 父母的礼物

3 词尾没有 s 的复数名词加 's → 名词所有格

Women's Day 妇女节

Children's Day 儿童节

4 表示商店、某人的家、教堂等，经常将名词所有格所修饰的词省略。

- There are a lot of old people in the **doctor's (office)**.
  这个诊所里有很多老人。
- The **hairdresser's (shop)** does good business.
  这家理发店的生意非常好。

5 表示几个名词共有的所属关系，只在最后一个名词后加"'s"；表示几个名词分别的所属关系，在每个名词后边分别加"'s"。

- **John and Jane's mother** is asking a bargain. 表示双方共同所有
  约翰和简的妈妈正在砍价。
- **John's and Jane's mothers** are asking a bargain. 表示双方各自所有
  约翰的妈妈和简的妈妈都在砍价。

用法

表示时间

yesterday's weather 昨天的天气

twenty **minutes'** break 二十分钟的休息

用在度量衡和价值后面

two **kilometers'** distance 两千米的距离

ten **dollars'** worth 价值十美元

用在集体名词后面

people's rights 人民的权力

用在表示天体的名词后面

the **sun's** light 太阳光

the **moon's** surface 月球表面

用在国家或城市后面

Canada's map 加拿大地图

用在固定表达中

on **one's** way home 某人回家的路

Exercise

一、根据图片和汉语提示，在空格处写上正确的答案。

1. _____ (wallet) 爸爸
的钱包

2. _____ (clothes) 婴
儿的衣服

3. _____ (smile) 姑姑
的笑容

4. _____ (barber) 去理发

5. _____ (books) 学生们
的书

6. _____ (cellphone) 尼
克的新手机

二、根据句意和提示词填空。

1. September 10th is _____ Day. 九月十日是教师节。

2. The watch was sent by _____. 这块手表是我爸爸的朋友送的。

3. I saw our math teacher went to the _____. (doctor) 我看到我们的数学老师去医院了。

4. _____ is fine. (weather) 今天天气晴朗。

5. — How far is it from the supermarket to the hospital? 从超市到医院有多远？

— _____ riding bike will take you there. 骑自行车 30 分钟就能到。

6. _____ need cleaning. (Bart, Dick) 巴特的房间和迪克的房间需要打扫。

7. Mary is _____ friend. (Linda, May) 玛丽是琳达和梅的朋友。

参考答案：

一、1. father's wallet　　2. baby's clothes　　3. aunt's smile　　4. go to the barber's

　　5. students' books　　6. Nick's new cellphone

二、1. Teachers'　　2. my father's friend　　3. doctor's　　4. Today's weather

　　5. Thirty minutes'　　6. Bart's and Dick's rooms　　7. Linda and May's

第八单元 名词的 of 所有格

of 所有格多用于指无生命的东西，表示所有关系，有时可与 's 所有格互换。

the name of the song
↓
the song's name
↓
这首歌的名字

the beginning of the movie
↓
the movie's beginning
↓
电影的开头

只能用 of 所有格的情况

意义	示例
当表示有生命东西的名词带有短语或从句作后置修饰语时	Do you know the class of the girl wearing a white skirt? 你知道那个穿白色短裙女孩的班级吗？
避免出现"所有格 + 所有格 + 名词"的结构时，必须用 of 所有格	I'll stay at the house of my mother's friend tonight. 我今晚将住在我妈妈的朋友的家里。
中心词是表示人的形容词时，用 of 所有格	You can't bear the misery of the poor. 你无法忍受穷人的悲惨生活。
表同位关系	She has worked in the country of China for 3 years. 她在中国工作三年了。

双重所有格

1 双重所有格是由"of + 's 所有格"共同构成，其中 's 所有格之后的名词被省略，双重所有格的形式也可以用"of + 名词性物主代词"。

of+'s 所有格
a book of my sister's
我姐姐的一本书

of+ 名词性物主代词
a book of hers
她的一本书

of 后的名词必须是人，而非物
Tom is a friend of my brother's.
汤姆是我哥哥的一个朋友。

2 双重所有格修饰的名词与指示代词 this，that，those，these 连用，通常表示爱憎、褒贬等感情色彩。

表示赞赏
• This daughter of your aunt's looks very nice.
　指示代词 + 双重所有格
你姑姑家的这个女儿真漂亮。

表示厌恶
• Those friends of Nemo's are not so polite.
　指示代词 + 双重所有格
尼莫的那些朋友并不那么礼貌。

3 **of** 之前的名词，通常与不定冠词 **a/an** 及 **some**，**any**，**several**，**few**，**no** 等表示数量的词或疑问形容词 **which** 连用，但不可与定冠词 **the** 连用。

- I have broken **a cup of the teacher's** in the school office.
  我在学校办公室打碎了老师的一个杯子。
- I invite **some classmates of my daughter's** to the party.
  我邀请了我女儿的一些同学来参加聚会。

4 双重所有格中 of 前的名词为 picture，photo，portrait，printing，statue 等时，并非指某人本人的肖像或照片，而是指该人所收藏的肖像或照片等。

画像不是"我爸爸"，是"我爸爸"所收藏的画像

- This is **a portrait of my father's**.
  这是我爸爸收藏的一张画像。

该画像上的人是"我爸爸"

- This is **a portrait of my father**.
  这是我爸爸的一张画像。

所有格还可以表示动作的执行者、动作的承受者、表示修饰关系。

The boss tries his best to meet the <u>staff's demands</u>.
动作的执行者
老板尽最大努力满足员工的要求。

<u>The children's education</u> plays an
　　　动作的承受者
important role in the development of our country.
孩子的教育对我们国家的发展有重要的作用。

Our company only employs people of
<u>doctor's degree</u>.
　修饰关系
我们公司只招聘有博士学位的人。

 **Exercise**

写出下列句子的同义句。

1. The girl's name is Rose. _____

2. This is a CD of Jack's. _____

3. Miss White is a friend of my mother's. _____

4. *Harry Potter* is one of Mary's books. _____

5. Nelson's birthday is in May. Georgy's birthday is in May, too. _____

参考答案：

1. The name of the girl is Rose.
2. This is Jack's CD.
3. Miss White is one of my mother's friends.
4. *Harry Potter* is a book of Mary's.
5. Nelson's and Georgy's birthdays are in May.

第三章

代词
Pronouns

第一单元 人称代词

为了避免重复，有的时候会使用人称代词来代指前面提过的人或事物。人称代词有主格、宾格之分。

用法

1 人称代词的主格在句中作主语。I 无论放在哪个位置都要保持大写。**you** 单复数同形，具体的意义要根据上下文决定。

- **We** are students in a senior high school.
  主格
  我们是一所高中的学生。

- Are **you** a nurse?
  表示单数"你"
  你是一名护士吗？

- **You** really give me a big surprise.
  表示复数"你们"
  你们真的给了我一个大大的惊喜。

- **She** is good at playing the piano, but **I**
  主格   句中大写
  am not.
  她擅长弹钢琴，但我不行。

2 人称代词的宾格在句中作动词或介词的宾语。

宾格 us 作动词 told 的宾语

- The teacher **told us**, "You should help **each other**".
  老师告诉我们"你们应该互相帮助"。

  相互代词是表示相互关系的代词，它没有复数形式，只有名词性质，可以加 -'s 构成所有格，表示所属关系，可以用作定语。英语中有两组相互代词：each other 和 one another。

- She takes good care **of him**.
  宾格 him 作介词 of 的宾语
  她把他照顾得很好。

3 对于动物的指代，单数用 **it**，复数用 **they**，有的时候也会用 **he** 或者 **she** 来指代，含有一定的感情色彩。

- Every time I got home; my pet dog welcomed me. **He** knew that I came back.
  此处指 pet dog，含有感情色彩
  每次我到家的时候，我的宠物狗就会来迎接我。他知道我回来了。

顺序

1 单数人称代词同时出现，顺序是：第二人称、第三人称、第一人称。

- **You**, **she** and **I** work here over three years.
  你、她和我在这儿工作超过三年了。

2 复数人称代词同时出现，顺序是：第一人称、第二人称、第三人称。

- **We**, **you** and **they** live in the same city.
  我们、你们和他们居住在同一个城市。

3 在"及物动词＋副词"的结构中，作宾语的人称代词要放在动词和副词之间，而名词放在副词之前或者之后都可以。

- Can you help me **switch it off**?
  你能帮我关掉它吗？

- Please **put on your coat**.
  Please **put your coat on**.
  请穿上你的外套。

 **Exercise**

一、从下面四个选项中选出最佳答案。

1. The doctor asked _____ to open his mouth.

   A. he   B. her   C. him   D. she

2. My mother has a cat. _____ accompanies _____ to do everything.

   A. She; she   B. She; her   C. Her; her   D. it; she

3. Have you noticed the opening windows? Please close _____.

   A. it   B. them   C. its   D. it's

4. _____ want you to tell _____ something about _____.

   A. I; me; him   B. I; I; he   C. I; me; he   D. I; I; him

5. _____ go to school by school bus.

   A. We   B. He   C. She   D. it

6. _____, _____ and _____ don't study at the same school.

   A. You; they; we   B. They; we; you   C. We; you; they

7. My mother is a good teacher. _____ is kind to students.

   A. He   B. She   C. Her   D.him

8. Miss Green teaches _____ French.

   A. we   B. she   C. us   D. our

二、找出下面句子的错误之处并改正。

1. Jim met some friends. Them are good at sports. _____

2. Me didn't know the man in blue. _____

3. Mark lives in Germany. I am happy to receive letters from he. _____

4. The salesman tried to persuade I to buy the shoes. _____

5. She are going to go hiking this Friday. _____

参考答案：

一、1. C   2. B   3. B   4. A   5. A   6. C   7. B   8. C

二、1. Them → They   2. Me → I   3. he → him   4. I → me   5. are → is

第二单元 物主代词

物主代词指的是表示所有关系的代词，也是人称代词的所有格形式。物主代词有两种：形容词性物主代词和名词性物主代词。

人称	第一人称		第二人称		第三人称			复数
数	单数	复数	单数	复数	单数			复数
形容词性物主代词	my	our	your	your	his	her	its	their
名词性物主代词	mine	ours	yours	yours	his	hers	its	theirs
汉语意思	我的	我们的	你的	你们的	他的	她的	它的	他/她/它们的

1 形容词性物主代词相当于形容词，在句中只能作定语。

- **My** cousin is an excellent basketball player.
  我的堂弟是一名优秀的篮球运动员。
- **His** parents don't allow him to play computer games.
  他的父母不允许他玩电脑游戏。

2 形容词性物主代词与 **own** 连用表示强调。

- All kids have **their** own ideas about Christmas.
  每个孩子对圣诞节都有自己的想法。
- I'll finish the task on **my** own.
  我会自己完成任务。

3 形容词性物主代词有时只是出于意义表达的需要，而并不强调所属关系。

- It's your fault, and you should try **your** best to make up for her.
  这是你犯的错，你应该尽最大努力弥补她。
- On **my** way home, I met the Greens.
  在回家的路上，我遇见了格林一家。

4 名词性物主代词相当于名词，等同于"形容词性物主代词 + 名词"，在句中可以作主语、宾语和表语。

- **My** bag is bigger than **yours**.
  我的袋子比你的大。
- **Our** houses are on the first floor, and **theirs** are on the third floor.
  我们的房子在一楼，他们的在三楼。

5 用于"of+ 名词性物主代词"的双重所有格结构中，表示"其中之一"，或者是某种感情色彩。

- I'll recommend a professor of **mine** to give you some advice.
  我会推荐一位我的导师给你一些建议。
- What if they share the food of **theirs**?
  如果他们给我们分享他们的食物怎么办？

6 冠词 a/an/the 和 this/that/some 等词后不能再加物主代词或所有格。

(×) **The her** speech is unforgettable.

(√) **Her** speech is unforgettable.

她的演讲令人难忘。

(×) My friend lends me **a his** pen.

(√) My friend lends me **a** pen.

我的朋友借给我一支笔。

7 谓语动词要和名词性物主代词所指代的名词保持一致。

- Our **parents** are Americans, while theirs **are** Englishmen.

我们的父母是美国人，他们的父母是英国人。

- His **house** is clean, but mine **is** dirty.

他的房子很整洁，但我的房子很脏。

Exercise

从下面的方框中选出合适的代词填入空格处。

---

my   your   mine   his   her   their   theirs   our

---

1. These toys are not _____. They belong to Mike. 这些玩具不是我的。它们属于迈克。

2. Where're _____ socks? 我的袜子在哪？

3. This is _____ pencil and _____ is on the desk. 这是你的铅笔，他的铅笔在桌子上。

4. The students went to P.E. class. _____ coats remain in the classroom. 学生去上体育课了。他们的外套留在教室。

5. _____ bed is bigger than _____. 我们的床比他们的大。

6. They lend us a computer of _____. 他们借给了我们一台他们的电脑。

7. What does _____ father do? 你爸爸是做什么工作的？

8. Maria is my little sister. My grandma often sends _____ to school. 玛利亚是我妹妹。我外祖母经常送她上学。

9. All of us love _____ head teacher. 我们所有人都爱我们的校长。

10. _____ twin brother is a lawyer in a law firm. 他的双胞胎哥哥是一家律所的律师。

参考答案：

1. mine   2. my   3. your; his   4. Their   5. Our; theirs

6. theirs   7. your   8. her   9. our   10. His

第三单元 反身代词

反身代词常用于表示某人自己。比如：我自己、你自己、他自己、他们自己等。反身代词有单、复数之分，单数通常以 **self** 结尾，复数通常以 **selves** 结尾。

1 反身代词表示某人自己，可在句中作动词、介词的宾语。

· The young man thinks highly of **himself**.
这个年轻人对自己评价颇高。

· The baby saw **itself** from the mirror for the first time.
这个婴儿第一次从镜子中看到自己。

2 反身代词可用在 be，feel，look 等系动词后作表语。

· You **are** not **yourself** today.
你今天状态不好。

· She **looks herself** beautiful.
她自己看起来漂亮极了。

3 反身代词可用于表示强调，一般出现在名词、代词的主格形式后面，或在句尾作同位语。

· Even Alice **herself** was unclear about the matter.
即使爱丽丝本人对这件事也不清楚。

· My little brother went to school **himself** today.
我弟弟今天自己去了学校。

4 反身代词要和所指代的名词、代词在人称和数上保持一致。

· I **myself** have no idea about the work.
我自己对这份工作毫无头绪。

· He **himself** runs three shops in two years.
他自己在两年之内开了三家店。

5 反身代词不能单独在句中作主语，但当 and，or，but，neither ... nor ... 连接两个并列的主语时，第二个主语可以用反身代词，通常是指 **myself** 或 **ourselves**。

· Teachers and **ourselves** will plant trees in the park next Friday.
我们和老师下周五去公园植树。

· My father and **myself** went fishing at that time.
那时我和我爸爸去钓鱼了。

6 反身代词出现在一些固定短语中。

help **oneself** 自便，自取
enjoy **oneself** 玩得开心
in **oneself** 本身
by **oneself** 独自
between **ourselves** 私密的
come to **oneself** 恢复知觉

 **Exercise**

一、按要求在空格处写出对应的代词形式。

1. he（反身代词）_____

2. I（反身代词）_____

3. we（形容词性物主代词）_____

4. he（人称代词的宾格）_____

5. she（反身代词）_____

6. we（反身代词）_____

7. they（名词性物主代词）_____

8. you（形容词性物主代词）_____

9. they（反身代词）_____

10. I（名词性物主代词）_____

11. you（反身代词）_____

12. we（名词性物主代词）_____

二、从右边的方框中选出合适的反身代词填在空格处。

1. The little girl can dress _____.

2. People enjoyed _____ in the park.

3. Help _____ to some fruit after lunch.

4. The boy teaches _____ Spanish.

5. You should learn how to take care of _____.

6. The music _____ is very popular among the youth.

7. My aunt can mend the clothes _____.

8. Let's clean up the room _____.

9. I must improve _____ in writing during this semester.

10. I met a man speaking to _____ on the bus.

> yourself
>
> myself
>
> themselves
>
> herself
>
> ourselves
>
> himself
>
> itself

参考答案：

一、1. himself 2. myself 3. our 4. him 5. herself 6. ourselves 7. theirs
　　8. your 9. themselves 10. mine 11. yourself/yourselves 12. ours

二、1. herself 2. themselves 3. yourself 4. himself 5. yourself
　　6. itself 7. herself 8. ourselves 9. myself 10. himself

第四单元　不定代词 1：some, any; no, no one, none

some, any

1 some 常用于肯定句中，any 常用于否定句、疑问句和条件句中。

- There are **some** apples in the bag.
  袋子里有一些苹果。
- I didn't have **any** money in my wallet.
  我的钱包里没钱了。
- Do you still have **any** questions about the machine?
  关于这台机器，你还有什么问题吗？

2 在表示请求或建议的疑问句中，常用 some 表达期望得到对方的肯定回答。

- Could you give me **some** advice about tomorrow's test?
  你能就明天的考试给我一些建议吗？

3 在肯定句中，有时也可用 any 表示"任何"的含义。

- You can call me at **any** time.
  你可以在任何时间打给我。
- You can try on **any** clothes if you like.
  你可以试穿任何一件你喜欢的衣服。

4 any 可以和含有否定意义的副词连用，强调句子否定。

- He can answer the question **without any** hesitation.
  他可以毫不犹豫地回答出这个问题。
- She can **hardly** offer **any** help to us.
  她给我们提供不了任何帮助。

no, no one, none

1 no 的意思是"无，没有"，只有形容词性质，在句中作定语，既可指人，也可指物。no 既可修饰单、复数可数名词，也可修饰不可数名词。

- **No student** wants to be the monitor of the class. 没有学生想成为这个班级的班长。
- There is **no wine** in the cups.
  杯子里没有酒了。

2 no one 只能单独使用，后边不能接 of 短语，只能指人。no one 作主语时，谓语动词用单数形式。

- There **is no one** in the classroom.
  教室里没有人。
- **No one wants** to speak firstly.
  没有人想第一个发言。

3 none 的意思是"没有人，没有东西"，在句中可以作主语、宾语和表语。none of 后边可以跟复数代词、可数名词复数以及不可数名词，后接代词或可数名词复数时，谓语动词可用单数，也可用复数；后接不可数名词时，谓语动词用单数。

- There is **none** in the cupboard.
  橱柜里什么也没有。
- **None of them** agrees/agree with this idea. 他们中没有人同意这个主意。
- **None of the food** is free today.
  今天的食物不免费。

 **Exercise**

一、根据要求改写句子。

1. There is some milk in the bottle. （改为否定句）

_____

2. Julia makes some friends in the new school. （改为否定句）

_____

3. There is some water for the little panda. （改为一般疑问句）

_____

4. Her mother didn't leave any money for her. （改为肯定句）

_____

5. Yes, please give me a glass of beer. （写出问句）

_____

二、请用 no, no one, none 的正确形式填空。

1. _____ them can cook fish. 他们中没有人会做鱼。

2. There is _____ in the supermarket. 超市里没有人。

3. He took _____ when traveling. 他旅行的时候什么也没有带。

4. There is _____ paper in the toilet. 厕所没有纸了。

5. _____ them are civil servants. 他们中没有人是公务员。

6. He will tell _____ about the bad news. 他不会告诉任何人这个坏消息。

7. There is _____ answer to this question. 这个问题没有答案。

8. _____ the money in that card belongs to me. 卡里没有一分钱是我的。

9. — Which one do you like, car, money or house? 车、钱和房子，你喜欢哪个？

    — _____. 都不喜欢。

参考答案：

一、1. There isn't any milk in the bottle.

　　2. Julia doesn't make any friends in the new school.

　　3. Is there any water for the little panda?

　　4. Her mother left some money for her.

　　5. Would you like some beer?

二、1. None of　　2. no one

　　3. none　　4. no

　　5. None of　　6. no one

　　7. no　　8. None of

　　9. None

第五单元 不定代词 2：every，each；both，all

every, each

1 **every** 指三者或三者以上的人或物。**each** 指两者或两者以上的人或物。

- I'll keep **every** word my grandma said in my mind.

  我会记下奶奶说的每一句话。

- They plant trees in **each** side of the road.

  他们在道路的两旁种上了树。

2 **every** 具有形容词的属性，不可单独使用。**each** 可以作代词也可以作形容词。

- **Every** worker works hard in the factory.

  每个工人都在工厂里努力工作。

- **Each** of us received a letter from Santa Claus.

  我们两个人都收到了圣诞老人的信。

- Jenny prepared gifts for **each** kid.

  珍妮给每个孩子准备了礼物。

3 **every** 强调整体概念，而 **each** 强调个体概念。

- **Every** player in our team is strong.

  我们队的所有运动员都很强壮。

- **Each** boy wants to be the champion.

  每个男孩都想当冠军。

4 **every** 与 **not** 连用，表示部分否定；而 **each** 和 **not** 连用，表示全部否定。

- **Not every** could pass the test easily.

  并不是每个人都能很容易地通过考试。

- **Each** of them would **not** call you.

  他们都不会给你打电话的。

5 **every** 可以表示"每逢，每隔"的含义；而 **each** 没有此意。

- We send an E-mail to each other **every** Friday.

  我们每周五给对方发一封邮件。

- You should take medicine **every** three hours.

  你应该每隔三小时吃一次药。

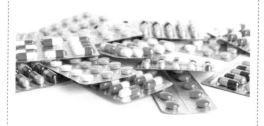

both, all

1 **all** 指三者或三者以上的人或物。

- **All** of us support him to be the leader.

  我们都支持他当领导。

- **All** the girls cleaned the windows of the classroom after school.

  所有的女孩在放学后擦教室的窗户。

2 all 修饰单数名词时，谓语动词用单数；修饰复数名词时，谓语动词用复数；修饰不可数名词时，谓语动词用单数。

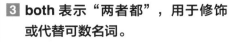

- **All** the water runs out.
  所有的水都用完了。
- **All** the kids go to bed at 8:00 p.m. in the kindergarten.
  在幼儿园，所有的孩子晚上八点上床睡觉。

3 both 表示"两者都"，用于修饰或代替可数名词。

- The wounded man lost **both** legs forever.
  这个伤员永远地失去了双腿。
- **Both** my sister **and** I feel relaxed.
  我姐姐和我都感觉很放松。

 **Exercise**

为下列句子勾选出正确的答案。

1. These bottles are worth 10 cents ○ **each** ○ **every**.

2. ○ **All** ○ **Both** my father and mother work in the hospital.

3. ○ **Every** ○ **Each** of the firemen will not leave at this dangerous time.

4. We two study in the same school. ○ **Both** ○ **All** of us leave school at 4:30 p.m.

5. We burst into tears when we saw ○ **every** ○ **each** other.

6. ○ **All** ○ **Both** is eager to know what happened.

7. This baby slept ○ **both** ○ **all** day.

8. Not ○ **every** ○ **each** has a chance to succeed.

9. ○ **All** ○ **Both** Lucy and Lily have long straight hair.

10. The metro runs ○ **each** ○ **every** 8 minutes.

参考答案：
1. each 2. Both 3. Each 4. Both 5. each
6. All 7. all 8. every 9. Both 10. every

第六单元 不定代词 3：either，neither，nor；one，another，the other，others

either, neither, nor

1 either 表示"两者中的任何一个"，可用作代词或形容词。

• — Which one do you prefer, rice or noodles?
  你更喜欢米饭还是面条？

  — **Either** is OK. 任何一个都可以。

• There are two keys of this room and you can take away **either** of them.
  有两把这个房间的钥匙，你可以拿走任何一把。

2 neither 表示"两者都不"，可用作代词或形容词。

• **Neither** of the couple can drive a car.
  夫妻两人都不会开车。

• **Neither** of us will attend the meeting.
  我们两个人都不会出席会议。

3 either 和 neither 可分别构成短语 either ... or ... 和 neither ... nor ...，谓语动词采用就近原则。

• **Neither** I **nor she wants** to be a teacher.
  我和她都不想成为一名老师。

• **Either** he **or I want** to go to the cinema.
  他和我都想去看电影。

4 neither，nor 都可以用于省略结构中，表示"也不"，构成并列的否定成分。

• He can't swim; **neither/nor** can his sister.
  他不会游泳，他妹妹也不会。

• They did not go to school on Monday, **nor** on Tuesday.
  他们周一没有去上学，周二也没有去。

one, the other, another, others

1 在一定范围内的两人（物），一个用 one，另一个用 the other，即为 one ... the other ...。

• I have two balloons. **One** is pink, **the other** is yellow.
  我有两个气球。一个是粉色的，一个是黄色的。

2 other 是形容词性质，后边加名词复数。

• **Other** children are running.
  其他的孩子在跑。

• **Other** people are waiting for the bus.
  其他人正在等公交车。

3 another 泛指三者以上中的另一个。

• This pair of shoes doesn't fit and I want to try **another** one.
这双鞋子不合适，我想试试另外一双。

• I want **another** orange.
我想再要一个橘子。

4 泛指别的人或物，用 others。在一定范围内，除去一部分人或物，指代剩余的全部用 the others（相当于 the rest）。

• We're not allowed to chat with **others** in the class.
我们不被允许在课堂上和其他人聊天。

• Some bananas are good, while **the others** are bad.
一些香蕉是好的，其他的是坏的。

从下列选项中，选出最佳答案填在空格处。

A. another   B. either   C. the other   D. neither   E. others
F. neither ... nor ...   G. one   H. the others

1. _____ of my two little brothers passed the exam.

2. I prepared two Christmas cards. _____ is for the math teacher, _____ is for my best friend.

3. Could you give me _____ ten minutes to fill the blanks?

4. You can learn a lot in working with _____.

5. Some apples are sweet, while _____ are sour.

6. _____ you _____ she is equal to this position.

7. These two skirts are same in price and style, and you can choose _____ one.

8. This fridge doesn't work well. I need to buy a new _____.

参考答案：
1. D   2. G; C   3. A   4. E   5. H   6. F   7. B   8. G

第七单元 不定代词 4：many，much；few，a few，little，a little

many, much

many 和 much 都表示"许多"，可以用于固定短语中。many 用于修饰可数名词，much 用于修饰不可数名词。

many houses 许多房子

· **Many** houses have been built during the ten years.

这十年间，这里建造了许多房屋。

much money 许多钱

· My uncle earned **much** money this year.

我叔叔今年赚了很多钱。

few, a few, little, a little

	修饰可数名词		修饰不可数名词	
肯定意义	a few 一些	—	a little 一些	—
否定意义	—	few 几乎没有	—	little 几乎没有
作用	不强调具体的数量，兼具名词和形容词的性质。在句中作主语、宾语、定语，用作名词时，可以与 of 一起构成 of 短语。			

a few 修饰可数名词，含有肯定意义

· I passed the math examination **a few days** ago.

几天前我通过了数学测试。

few 修饰可数名词，含有否定意义

· **Few people** were willing to give up this chance.

几乎没有人愿意放弃这次机会。

· **A few of them** gave us a hand.

他们中的一些人帮助了我们。

a little 修饰不可数名词，含有肯定意义

· She only had **a little** soup for dinner.

她晚餐只喝一些汤。

little 修饰不可数名词，含有否定意义

· There is **little water** to use.

几乎没有水可以用。

· He knows **little of** music, so he has to keep silence.

他对音乐知之甚少，所以他不得不保持沉默。

比较：a little 和 a bit

a little 与 a bit 都可以表示"有点儿"，两者有时可互换，语气要比 rather 弱很多。

a little 可直接修饰不可数名词，a bit 不能直接修饰，需要采用"a bit + of + 名词"的形式：

（×）a bit wine 一点儿酒
（√）a little wine 一点儿酒
（√）a bit of wine 一点儿酒

另外，两者的否定结构区别很大：

not a little 非常，许多
not a bit = not at all 一点也不

一、下面方框中有可数名词也有不可数名词，请仔细甄别哪些可以和 **much** 连用，哪些可以和 **many** 连用，并将其填在对应的框中。

> worker, tea, meat, boy, doctor, work, children, money, flower,
> rice, mutton, chair, fun, failure, friend, time, table, penguin,
> information, tomato, butter, traffic, problem, coffee

much	many

二、判断下列句子中的代词使用是否正确，正确的在括号里写（**T**），错误的在括号里写（**F**）。

1. You've drank many wine at the banquet. （　）

2. Louise said that he has too many work to do. （　）

3. A little people are doing exercise in the park. （　）

4. Hurry up. We have few minutes left. （　）

5. My grandpa bought me a camera a few days ago. （　）

6. I couldn't afford it. Because I have a little money. （　）

7. Maybe you can drink little wine. （　）

8. Few people like to eat durian. （　）

9. Only a few students can meet the requirement. （　）

10. Please give little water to these flowers every day when I am on a business trip. （　）

参考答案：
一、much: tea, meat, work，money, rice, mutton, fun, failure, time, information, butter, traffic, coffee
many: worker, boy, doctor, children, flower, chair, friend, table, penguin, tomato, problem
二、1. F　2. F　3. F　4. T　5. T　6. F　7. F　8. T　9. T　10. F

第八单元 不定代词5：复合代词

1 -one 和 -body 类的复合不定代词指人，-thing 类的复合不定代词指物，-where 类的复合不定代词指地点。

· **Everyone** had a smile on their faces.

每个人脸上带着笑容。

· He knows **nothing** about it.

他对这件事情一无所知。

· You can see the crowd **everywhere** on holidays.

假期里到处都是人群。

2 some，any 开头的复合不定代词的用法和 some，any 一致。some- 用在肯定句中，any- 用在否定句和疑问句中。

· **Someone** left the package in front of the police station.

有人在警局前面丢下了这个包裹。

· She didn't know **anyone** in the company.

她不认识公司里的人。

3 any- 类的复合不定代词表示"任何……"的时候，可以用在肯定句中。在表示想要得到肯定回答的疑问句中，可以使用 some- 类的复合不定代词。

· — Would you like **something** to drink?

你想要一点喝的吗？

· — **Anything** is Okay.

任何东西都可以。

4 复合不定代词在句子中作主语时，谓语要用单数形式。

· **Everyone shows** great interest to this auction.

大家都对这次拍卖展示了极大的兴趣。

· **Nobody lives** up to the boss's expectations.

没有人达到老板的期待。

5 形容词如果修饰复合不定代词，要放在复合不定代词的后面。

· The man has **something important** to tell us.

这个人有重要的事告诉我们。

· There is **nothing wrong** with your car.

你的车没出毛病。

比较：some one 和 someone

some one 既可指人也可指物，可以和介词 of 搭配使用。

someone 只可指人，不能和介词 of 搭配使用。

any one 和 anyone，every one 和 everyone 的用法与之同理。

<u>**Someone**</u> parks the car on the road.
　　指人

有人把车停在了路上。

I like **some one** of the books.

我喜欢其中的一本书。

请将左边的代词与右边的词汇组合成一个你需要的复合代词填在相应的位置，并将其补充在句子里面。

some	any	every	no		one	body	thing	where

_____ + _____ = _____   _____ + _____ = _____

_____ + _____ = _____   _____ + _____ = _____

_____ + _____ = _____   _____ + _____ = _____

_____ + _____ = _____   _____ + _____ = _____

_____ + _____ = _____   _____ + _____ = _____

1. We bought _____, because the shops were closed. 我们什么也没有买，因为商店都关门了。

2. If you have enough time and money, you can go _____ you want. 如果你有足够的时间和金钱，你可以去任何你想去的地方。

3. _____ should contribute to the protection of the environment. 每个人都应该为保护环境贡献一份力量。

4. _____ cares what you said. 没有人会在乎你说了什么。

5. I want to be a rich man and help _____ who needs help. 我想成为一个有钱人，帮助那些有需要的人。

6. I couldn't hear the voice, and there must be _____ wrong with my ears. 我不能听到声音，我的耳朵肯定有问题了。

7. Is there _____ I can do for you? 我能为你做些什么吗？

8. The boy had _____ to hide in the heavy rain. 这个男孩没有地方躲避大雨。

9. I promise that I will not leak the secret to _____. 我承诺，我不会泄露这个秘密给任何人。

10. We've walked for a long time. Let's find _____ to have a rest! 我们已经走了很久了。找个地方休息一下吧！

参考答案：
1. nothing   2. anywhere   3. Everyone/Everybody   4. No one/Nobody   5. someone
6. something   7. anything   8. nowhere   9. anyone/anybody   10. somewhere

第九单元 指示代词

指示代词是用来指示或标识人或事物的代词，所指代的对象取决于说话者和听话者共同熟悉的语言环境。

this, that, these, those

1 **this** 和 **these** 表示在时间上或空间上较近的人或物。

- **This** is my car.

  这是我的车。

- Lisa got married with John **these** days.

  丽萨最近和约翰结婚了。

2 **that** 和 **those** 表示在时间上或空间上较远的人或物。

- **That** is my daughter.

  那个人是我的女儿。

- **Those** students haven't finished their homework.

  那些学生没有完成作业。

3 指示代词在句中可以作主语、宾语、表语和定语。

- Can you do **this** by your own?

  　　　　　宾语

  你能自己做这个吗？

- **These** beggars grabbed food in a panic.

  定语

  这些乞丐在慌乱中抢到了食物。

4 **this** 和 **that** 有时也可用于代替整个句子或句中的一部分。

- Tom ate a lot of bread. **That** is why he didn't feel hungry.

  汤姆吃了许多面包。这就是为什么他不饿。

5 指示代词 **that** 和 **those** 可用于代替前面已提到的人或事，但 **this** 和 **these** 无此用法。

- Bob explained the **reason** why he got late, and **that** made sense.

  鲍勃解释了他迟到的原因，这就讲得通了。

- Tony **failed in the final examination and was criticized by teacher**; **those** makes him unconfident.

  托尼期末考试考砸了，受到了老师的批评。这些使他变得不自信。

such, same

1 **such** 用作名词性质，可以作主语，也可以作宾语或是表语；可以是单数意义，也可以是复数意义；常与 **as** 连用。

- **Such are** our opinions on our wedding.

  这就是我们关于婚礼的意见。

- He has always regarded **as such**.

  他一直都是这样认为的。

2 **such** 用作形容词性质，多作前置定语，修饰不可数名词和可数名词单复数。修饰单数可数名词时，要与不定冠词 **a** 或 **an** 连用。

- I've never seen **such a** lovely cat.

  我从没见过如此漂亮的猫。

- Kate is **such a** warm-hearted person.

  凯特是一个如此热心肠的人。

3 same 相当于形容词时，在句中作定语。same 常和 as，that 连用。

- We waste too much time on the **same** thing.
  我们在同一件事上浪费了太多时间。
- I have the **same** book **as** yours.
  我有一本和你一样的书。

4 same 相当于名词时，在句中作主语、宾语、表语，可表示单数或者复数。

- It seems that they think the **same** about this problem.
  看起来他们对这个问题的看法是相同的。
- The twin brothers always do the **same** in the same situation.
  这对双胞胎兄弟总是在相同的情况下做出同样的事情。

 Exercise

将下列句子改写为复数形式，并翻译其汉语意思。

1. This is my notebook.

_____

2. What's that?

_____

3. That cute penguin is ill.

_____

4. It is a black and white dog.

_____

5. This is a bike my grandpa bought for me.

_____

参考答案：

1. These are my notebooks. 这些是我的笔记本。

2. What are those? 那些是什么？

3. Those cute penguins are ill. 那些可爱的企鹅生病了。

4. They are black and white dogs. 它们是黑白相间的狗。

5. These are bikes my grandpa bought for me. 这些是我爷爷给我买的自行车。

第十单元 疑问代词

疑问代词指表示疑问的代词，在句中用于提问，构成疑问句，没有单数和复数之分。

what 什么	who 谁（主格）
whom 谁（宾格）	whose 谁的
which 哪一个	

1 疑问代词常常放在句子的最前面，在句中可作主语、宾语、表语等。

- **Which** one is Lucy's coat?
  主语

  哪一件是露西的外套？

- **What** do you like?
  宾语

  你喜欢什么？

- **Whom** are you taking care of?
  宾语

  你在照顾谁？

- **Whose** toys are over there?
  定语

  谁的玩具在那儿？

- **Who** are you?
  表语

  你是谁？

除 who，whom 之外，疑问代词没有主格和宾格的变化。whom 是 who 的宾格，在书面语中通常用作动词宾语或介词宾语。在口语中，whom 作宾语时可以用 who 代替，但在介词后只能用 whom。

2 疑问代词在句中没有人称和数的变化。

- **What** are your hobbies?

  你有什么爱好？

- **Who** is your best friend?

  你最好的朋友是谁？

3 疑问代词 who，what，which 可与 ever 连用，构成复合疑问代词 whoever，whatever，whichever，常用来加强语气。

- **Whatever** gift you ask for, I'll buy it for you.

  无论你要什么礼物，我都会买给你。

- **Whoever** does well in study, parents will be happy.

  无论是谁考得好，父母都会很开心。

4 不管是疑问代词还是限定词，which 和 what 所强调的范围是不一样的。which 有一定的范围，what 没有限定的范围。

- **Which** kind of drinks do you like, wine or soft drinks?

  你喜欢哪种饮品，酒还是软饮料？

- **What** animals do you like?

  你喜欢什么动物？

5 疑问代词也可用来引导名词性从句，如：主语从句、宾语从句、表语从句和同位语从句。

- The man <u>who wears a black hat</u> is a
  　　　　定语从句

  thief.

  这个带着黑色帽子的男人是小偷。

- That is <u>what I requested</u>.
  　　　　表语从句

  那就是我所要求的。

6 疑问代词也能对介词宾语进行提问。疑问代词和介词可以一起放在句首，这种情况常出现在过去的文体中。现代英语中，常把疑问代词置于句首，介词放在句末。

- **About what** are you talking?
  介词、疑问代词

  你们在谈论什么？

- **Who** do you want to buy something **for**?
  疑问代词　　　　　　　　　　　　　　　介词

  你想给谁买东西？

Exercise

用特殊疑问句对划线部分进行提问。

1. I play basketball with <u>John</u>.

_____

2. Lily likes <u>orange juice</u> best.

_____

3. <u>Bob</u> won the game in the end.

_____

4. We can see <u>monkeys, elephants and tigers</u> in the zoo.

_____

5. <u>Nick's</u> hat is on the table.

_____

参考答案：

1. Whom do you play basketball with?　　2. Which drink does Lily like best?

3. Who won the game in the end?　　4. What animals can you see in the zoo?

5. Whose hat is on the table?

第十一单元 代词 it

1 代替不确定的人或事物、性别不明的婴儿或动物。

- — Who is **it** outside?

  外面是谁？

- — It's Mary.

  我是玛丽。

- Look at the baby.

  It is so lovely.

  看这个婴儿，可爱极了。

- I keep a pet pig. I can take good care of **it**.

  我养了一只宠物猪。我能照顾好它。

2 指时间、距离、天气和自然现象等。

- — What time is **it**?

  现在几点了？

- — **It** is ten past ten.

  现在是十点十分。

- **It** is not far from the bus stop to the bookstore.

  从公交车站到书店的距离并不远。

- As soon as I got home, **it** rained heavily.

  我刚到家，天就下起了大雨。

3 代替前文已经提过的事物。

- You can see the **laptop** on the table, please bring **it** to me.

  你可以看到桌子上的笔记本电脑，请把它带来给我。

- I bought a new **storybook** and read **it** to my family.

  我买了一本新的故事书，并把它读给我的家人听。

4 构成强调句型 "It is + 被强调部分 + that/(who) + 其余部分"。

- **It is** the sports meeting **that** has to be postponed。

  运动会不得不推迟了。

- **It was** Amy **that/who** left the classroom at last.

  最后离开教室的是艾米。

5 作形式主语。

- **It** is not difficult to answer the question.

  形式主语　　　　　真正的主语

  回答这个问题并不难。

- **It**'s time to go to bed.

  形式主语　真正的主语

  是时候上床睡觉了。

 **Exercise**

一、从下列四个选项中选出最佳答案。

1. I found a cat near the dustbin. Can I take _____ home?

   A. to   B. it   C. its   D. them

2. I guess _____ is Maggie in the doorway.

   A. who   B. she   C. he   D.it

3. It was he _____ helped me a lot in my study.

   A. who   B. it   C. whom   D. which

4. I give a birthday card to Tom and he likes _____ very much.

   A. them   B. its   C. it   D. one

5. It is in the museum _____ the exhibition will take place.

   A. its   B. who   C. that   D. whom

二、根据要求改写句子。

1. To go climbing tomorrow is a good idea. （it 作形式主语）

2. The distance from the bus station to the hotel is ten kilometers. （it 指代距离）

3. Lucy helped him a lot at work. （it 强调句；强调 Lucy）

4. The weather is going to rain the day after tomorrow. （it 指代天气）

5. 他们认为没有必要再和他多说了。（翻译句子，it 作形式宾语）

参考答案：
一、1. B 2. D 3. A 4. C 5. C
二、1. It is a good idea to go climbing tomorrow.
　　2. It is ten kilometers from the bus station to the hotel.
　　3. It was Lucy that helped him a lot at work.
　　4. It's going to rain the day after tomorrow.
　　5. They think it no need talking with him anymore.

第四章

数量词
Quantifiers

第一单元 数词的表达

基数词

表达方法	示例		
1~12 是基数词表达是无规律的，需要单独记忆。	one 一 four 四 seven 七 ten 十	two 二 five 五 eight 八 eleven 十一	three 三 six 六 nine 九 twelve 十二
13~19 的基数词基本上是由"3~9 的基数词 + 后缀 teen"构成，但是 13、15 和 18 这三个基数词有些特别，并不是直接由 three, five 和 eight 加后缀 teen 构成的。	thirteen 十三 fifteen 十五 eighteen 十八		
20~90 这些整十的基数词基本上由"2~9 的基数词 + 后缀 ty"构成，但是若干基数词有所差别，需要注意其拼写。	twenty 二十 forty 四十 sixty 六十 eighty 八十	thirty 三十 fifty 五十 seventy 七十 ninety 九十	
21~99 的基数词由"整十的基数词 + 连字符 + 1~9 的基数词"构成。	twenty-one 二十一 thirty-three 三十三 eighty-nine 八十九		
整百的数词由"1~9 的基数词 + hundred"构成，如果数词不是整百，而是由"百位数、十位数和个位数"共同构成的，那么在百位数和十位数之间可以用 and 连接起来。	two hundred 二百 six hundred and thirty-five 六百三十五		
千位数由"1~9 的基数词 + thousand"构成，不是整千的数词同百位数的表达。	three thousand 三千 one thousand two hundred and fifty-seven 一千二百五十七		
百万和十亿的表达	million 百万	billion 十亿	

序数词

表达方法	示例
第 1 到第 3 的序数词需要单独记忆。	first 第一 second 第二 third 第三
第 4 到第 19 的序数词一般由 "4-19 的基数词 + 后缀 th" 构成。	fifth 第五 thirteenth 第十三
第 20 到第 90 的整十序数词一般是把十位数的基数词的末尾 y 变成 i，再加后缀 eth。	twentieth 第二十 fortieth 第四十
第 21 到第 99 的非整十序数词在表达上需要遵循：十位数是基数词，个位数是序数词，而十位数和个位数要用连字符连接起来。	fifty-fifth 第五十五 seventy-third 第七十三
多位数的整百 / 千序数词由 hundred/thousand 等加后缀 th，然后在前面加上有关的基数词即可。	four hundredth 第四百 eight hundredth 第八百 three thousandth 第三千
多位数的非整十序数词如果有十位数和个位数，就要遵循：个位数用序数词，前面的数用基数词，零用 and 来表示。	one hundred and eighth 第一百零八 seven hundred and twenty-first 第七百二十一 four thousand five hundred and forty-sixth 第四千五百四十六

1. dozen 可以表示 "十二，一打"，score 可以表示 "二十"，与基数词连用，没有复数形式；而 dozens of ...、scores of ... 则是表示 "许多……"。
He bought two **dozen** bottles of soft drinks.
他买了 24 瓶饮料。
This café is not large, with a **score** of seats.
这家咖啡厅不大，只有 20 个座位。
There are **dozens of** people waiting in line over there.
那里有许多人在排队。
2. hundreds、thousands、millions 的习惯用法是后面接 of 介词短语。
Thousands of young people have lost jobs since the outbreak of the epidemic.
自疫情爆发以来，成千上万的年轻人失去了工作。

第二单元 数词的作用

基数词的作用

基数词的作用	示例
在句中作主语	In his view, **three** can bring good luck to him. 在他看来，三可以给他带来好运。
在句中作宾语	There are many pencils and I just want **one**. 有许多铅笔，我只要一支。
在句中作表语	My little sister is **ten** this year. 我妹妹今年十岁。
在句中作定语	A volleyball team has **twelve** athletes. 一个排球队有十二名运动员。
在句中作同位语	We **four** come from different countries. 我们四个来自不同的国家。
特殊用法：在某种情况下，基数词可以充当序数词表示顺序。	Lesson **Five** 第五课 page **fifty-eight** 第五十八页

序数词的作用

序数词的作用	示例
在句中作主语	Look, the **fourth** is my son. 看！第四个是我儿子。
在句中作宾语	— Which one do you want? 　你想要哪一个？ — The black one is more suitable for me. I want the **second**. 　黑色的更适合我。我想要第二个。
在句中作表语	Lucas is the **first** to get up this morning. 卢卡斯是今天早晨第一个起床的。
在句中作定语	This was the **first** letter I received from Jack. 这是我收到的杰克写的第一封信。
在句中作同位语	Who is the doctor, the **third** in the picture? 这个医生是谁？就是照片上的第三个人。
在句中作状语	**First**, you should take a hot bath. 首先，你应该洗个热水澡。

Exercise

一、为下列句子勾选正确的答案。

1. The group consisted of ○ **fifteen** ○ **fifteenth** people.

2. We ○ **two** ○ **second** have known each other for more than a decade.

3. Open your book. Let's begin to learn Lesson ○ **Third** ○ **Three**.

4. Kate performed well on the final exam this semester, and she was the ○ **one** ○ **first** place in our class.

5. Count from left to right; the ○ **twelfth** ○ **twelve** boy is my brother.

二、在下面空格处填上合适的数词。

C: Customer   S: Saleswoman

S: Welcome to Women's Store. What can I do for you?

C: I want to buy 1. _____ coats. 2. _____ is for my daughter, the other is for myself.

S: How old is your daughter?

C: 3. _____ .（十三岁）

S: Okay. The costumes in this area are suitable for her.

C: How much is the pink coat?

S: 4. _____ dollars. （400 美元）

C: It is too expensive.

S: Maybe you can look at another one.

C: How about the 5. _____ in the 6. _____ row.（第二排第八个）

S: It has been popular recently, and it is not expensive.

C: Pack it for me please.

S: OK, wait a moment.

参考答案：

一、1. fifteen   2. two   3. three   4. first   5. twelfth

二、1. two   2. One   3. Thirteen   4. Four hundred   5. eighth   6. second

第三单元 用数词表示时间

1 世纪：定冠词 + 序数词 + **century**

the twenty-first century 二十一世纪

the nineteenth century 第十九世纪

2 年代：**in** + 定冠词 + 基数词表示的世纪 + 整十数 + **s**

in the 1860s 19 世纪 60 年代

in the 1980s 20 世纪 80 年代

表示某个年代的早期或晚期可以在定冠词之后加上 early/late，中期可以在年代前面加上 mid-。如：in the early 1960s（在 20 世纪 60 年代早期），in the mid-1960s（在 20 世纪 60 年代中期）。

3 月份：介词 + 表示月份的名词，中间不加定冠词。

• The summer holiday usually lasts **from July** to **August**.

暑假通常从七月持续到八月。

• My birthday is **in February**.

我的生日在二月。

4 日期：定冠词 + 序数词，表示具体的某一天要在定冠词前加上介词 **on**。

• The sports meeting will be held **on the fifth day of April**.

这场运动会将在 4 月 5 日举行。

• Mother's Day falls **on the second Sunday of May**.

母亲节在五月的第二个星期日。

5 时刻除了可以直接读数字，还有以下表达方式。

◎ 整点：基数词 + **o'clock**。

• The class begins at **8:00/eight** a.m.

8 点开始上课。

• We leave at **3:00/three** p.m.

我们下午 3 点离开。

◎ 半小时以内的分钟数：分钟数 + **past** + 小时数。十五分钟可以用 **a quarter**，半小时可以用 **half**，所以表示半点：**half** + **past** + 小时数。

• We go home at 5:04/**four past five** p.m.

我们在下午 5:04 回家。

• Hurry up! It is **a quarter past eight** now.

快点，现在是 8:15。

• I bet that you can't get in touch with him before **half past nine**.

我打赌，你 9 点半之前联系不上他。

◎ 超过半小时分钟数：60 减去分钟数 + **to** + 下一小时的数字。

• I received the package at **five to ten** a.m.

我 9:55 收到了包裹。

• The lady ordered her meal at **ten to twelve** a.m.

这位女士在 11:50 点餐了。

时刻的表达并不是固定的，也可以灵活使用。表示"在中午"，可以用 at twelve o'clock，也可以用 at noon。

Exercise

一、找出下列句子中的错误之处，并改正。

1. In the twenty century, China's economy lagged far behind other countries. _____

2. In the 1980, my family still lived in the old house. _____

3. We plan to visit the Great Wall July 6th. _____

4. The old man usually goes to bed on 7:00 p.m. _____

5. The winter begins from the October. _____

二、根据图片提示，在空格处填上正确的时间表达。

Lily's Day

1. Lily wakes up at _____.

2. She washes her face and has breakfast before _____.

3. The class is over at _____.

4. She goes back home by bus and has dinner with her family at _____.

5. After finishing her homework, she goes to sleep at _____.

参考答案：
一、 1. twenty → twentieth   2. 1980 → 1980s   3. July 前面加 on   4. on → at   5. 去掉 the
二、 1. 7:00 a.m./seven o'clock   2. 7:30 a.m./half past seven   3. 10:55 a.m./five to eleven
　　 4. 6:15 p.m./a quarter past six   5. 8:45 p.m./a quarter to nine

第四单元 倍数、分数、小数、百分数的表示方法

1 倍数

◎ 倍数 + as + 形容词 + as

· The population here is **twice as much as** there.

这里的人口是那里的两倍。

◎ 倍数 + the size (amount/length/width ...) + of

· The adult elephant is **three times the weight of** the little one.

这头成年大象体重是小象的三倍。

◎ 倍数 + 形容词 / 副词的比较级 + than

· Lucy is **ten times cleverer than** Mark.

露西比马克聪明十倍。

◎ by + 倍数

· The number of freshmen has increased **by three times** this year.

今年的新生数量增加了三倍。

表示三倍或三倍以上的数量用 times 来表示，而表示两倍一般直接用 twice。

2 分数：分子用基数词，分母用序数词，当分子是大于一的数字时，序数词要用复数。

1/3 one third	1/6 one sixth
3/5 three fifth**s**	9/10 nine tenth**s**

· **One third** of students failed the exam.

三分之一的学生考试不及格。

3 小数：小数点左边的基数词要按照基数词的读法来读，但如果是三位或三位数以上，也可以一个个地读出来。小数点读作 **point**。小数点右边的数字需要一个个地读出来，其中"零"可以读作 **zero**。如果小数点左边的数字是零，则可省略不读，直接读小数点和后面的数字。

123.608 one hundred and twenty-three point six zero eight

0.0385 (zero) point zero three eight five

4 百分数通常是在阿拉伯数字后添加一个百分号 %，读为 **percent**。

· Nearly **eighty percent** people are dissatisfied with their current state of life.

近百分之八十的人不满足当前的生活状态。

5 数学运算

◎ 加：plus, and

· Two **plus/and** three is/equals five.

二加三等于五。

◎ 减：minus, from

· Six **minus** four equals two.

六减四等于二。

◎ 乘：multiplied by, times

· Three **times** nine is twenty-seven.

三乘以九等于二十七。

◎ 除：divided by, into

· Fifteen **divided by** three is five.

十五除以三等于五。

Exercise

一、在空格处填上合适的数词形式。

1. _____ of students are reluctant to go to boarding school.
   四分之三的学生不愿意上寄宿学校。

2. The math teacher taught us eight is _____ as much as four.
   数学老师教我们八是四的两倍。

3. Cindy was _____ away from winning the championship.
   辛迪差 1 秒就是冠军了。

4. More than _____ of middle school students are overweight.
   超过百分之六十的中学生过度肥胖。

二、写出下列句子的同义句。

1. Six and four is ten.

   _____

2. The little cow is three times heavier than that one.

   _____

3. Thirty-five divided by five is seven.

   _____

4. About ninety-five percent of the students wore uniforms.

   _____

5. About reforming the factory system, three quarters of the people were supportive.

   _____

参考答案：

一、1. Three-quarters　2. twice　3. 1 second　4. sixty percent/60%

二、1. Six plus four equals ten.　2. The little cow is four times the weight of that one.

3. Five into thirty-five is seven.

4. About five percent of the students didn't wear uniforms.

5. About reforming the factory system, a quarter of the workers opposed or abstained.

第五单元 量词

量词的分类

类别	量词	示例
表示个数	piece	a piece of news 一则新闻；a piece of paper 一篇论文
	item	an item of food 一种食物；an item of work 一项工作
	article	an article of clothes 一件衣服；an article of furniture 一件家具
表示形状	drop	a drop of oil 一滴油；a drop of rain 一滴雨
	bar	a bar of chocolate 一块巧克力；a bar of soap 一块肥皂
	slice	a slice of meat 一块肉；a slice of bread 一片面包
	lump	a lump of cheese 一块奶酪；a lump of sugar 一块糖
	flight	a flight of geese 一群大雁；a flight of steps 一段台阶
	head	a head of cabbage 一棵卷心菜；a head of sheep 一头羊
	bunch	a bunch of grapes 一串葡萄；a bunch of flowers 一束鲜花
	roll	a roll of paper 一卷纸；a roll of film 一卷胶卷
	block	a block of wood 一块木头；a block of ice 一块冰
	flood	a flood of moonlight 一滩月光；a flood of anger 满腔怒火
	cluster	a cluster of trees 一丛树；a cluster of flowers 一簇花
	swarm	a swarm of flies 一群苍蝇；a swarm of bees 一群蜜蜂
	beam	a beam of sunlight 一束阳光
	ball	a ball of fire 一团火；a ball of string 一团线
表示容量	bottle	a bottle of milk 一瓶牛奶；a bottle of wine 一瓶葡萄酒
	bowl	a bowl of rice 一碗大米；a bowl of noodles 一碗面条
	cup	a cup of tea 一杯茶；a cup of coffee 一杯咖啡
	glass	a glass of water 一杯水；a glass of milk 一杯牛奶
	spoonful	a spoonful of salt 一勺盐；a spoonful of honey 一勺蜂蜜
	mouthful	a mouthful of beer 一口啤酒；a mouthful of wine 一口葡萄酒
	bucket	a bucket of sand 一桶沙；a bucket of water 一桶水
	basket	a basket of bananas 一篮香蕉；a basket of food 一篮食物

量词的特点

1 有些量词词组修饰可数名词，有些量词词组修饰不可数名词，还有一些则两者都可修饰。

a **body of** regulations 一系列规定

a **herd of** sheep 一群羊

a **group of** ants 一群蚂蚁

a **sheet of** glass 一块玻璃

a **body of** hot wind 一股热风

a **crowd of** visitors 一群游客

2 有些量词词组相对灵活，有些则比较固定。

a **piece of** newspaper 一份报纸

a **piece of** bread 一片面包

a **piece of** jeans 一条牛仔裤

a **basket of** fruit 一篮子水果

a **basket of** cotton 一篮子棉花

3 根据其所表示的数或量可大致将量词词组分为四类，即：定量、不定量、大量、少量。

a **mouth of** water 一口水

a **bag of** rice 一袋大米

a **shred of** embarrassment 一丝尴尬

a **thrill of** joy 一阵喜悦

a **plenty of** rain 大量雨水

a **flood of** volunteers 一批志愿者

a **minority of** supporters 少数支持者

a **bite of** medicine 一点儿药

第五章

介词
Prepositions

第一单元 介词的分类

地点介词

above 在……之上	after 在……后面	against 倚着……	along 沿着
among 在……中间	around 围绕	at 在……处	before 在……前面
behind 在……后面	below 低于……	beside 在……旁边	between 在……之间
by 在……旁	down 在……下面	from 来自……	in 在……里面
inside 在……内部	near 靠近	on 在……上面	over 在……上方
under 在……下面			

- She sat **beside** him all night.
  她整晚都坐在他旁边。

- I left my phone **at** home.
  我把手机落在家了。

时间介词（短语）

about 大约	after 在……以后
at 在……时刻	before 在……以前
by 到……为止	during 在……期间
for 有……（之久）	from 从……起
in 在……时	on 在（某日）
since 自从	through 贯穿……期间
till 直到……	to 到（下一时刻）
until 直到……	ever since 自从

at the beginning of 在……开始时

at the end of 在……末尾

at the time of 在……时

- The building was destroyed **in** 1987.
  这座建筑于 1987 年被毁。

- We spent a long holiday **during** Spring Festival.
  我们在春节过了一个长假。

比较：

1. in 表示时间时，可以表示具体的年份、上下午、月份，还可以用在将来时中表示一段时间。而"after + 时间段"常用于表示过去时态的句子中。

2. on 表示时间时，表示具体的日期、节日等。

3. at 表示时间时，常表示一个时刻或瞬间。

4. since 表示时间时，常和现在完成时连用。for 也常和现在完成时连用，但它表示"总共有……时间"。

5. until 表示时间时常和 not 连用。

方向介词

across 横跨	against 对抗……	along 沿着	down 向下
for 向……	in 在……里面	into 进入	near 接近
through 穿过……	off 脱离，除	onto 到……上	over 跨过
past 超过	to 朝向……	towards 朝着	

- We plan to go **to** the museum on Saturday.
  我们打算周六去博物馆。
- You go **along** the street and turn right.
  你沿着这条街走，然后向右拐。

1. to 表示"朝向……"时，强调去的目的地，而 towards 则倾向于方向。
2. into 表示由外到里的过程，而 in 不强调这一点。into 和 in 后面都要接名词。

涉及介词

about 关于	besides 除了……还	except 除了……	for 就……而言
of ……的，有关……	on 关于，有关	to 对……而言	towards 针对
with 就……而言，对……来说			

- What's your opinion **on** this matter?
  你对这件事有什么看法？
- We work every day **except** weekends.
  除了周末，我们每天都工作。

方式介词

as 作为，当作	by 用；通过	in 用……（语言）	like 像……一样
on 骑；徒步；通过	over 通过（收音机）	through 通过	with 用……
without 没有……			

- **As** a student, you should study harder.
  作为一名学生，你应该更加努力学习。
- I go to school **by** bike.
  我骑自行车去上学。

比较：
by 主要用来表示乘坐交通工具，或用于被动语态。
with 表示使用具体的工具或手段。
in 表示使用的某种语言或文字。

目的介词

for 为了…… from 阻止…… to 为了……
- She fought **for** freedom.
  她为自由而战。

其他介词

所属介词：of ……的
让步介词：despite 尽管
　　　　　 in spite of 不管……

第二单元 介词短语的位置和作用

介词短语的位置

1 表示时间或地点的介词短语通常用作状语，可以放在句首或句尾。但要注意，放在句首时通常要用逗号和后面的内容隔开。

• We had a great time **in America**.

= **In America,** we had a great time.

我们在美国玩得很开心。

• There will be a great party **on May 6th**.

= **On May 6th,** there will be a great party.

5 月 6 日将会有一个很棒的聚会。

2 表示方向、方式、伴随、涉及、原因、目的的介词短语通常要放在句尾。

表示方向的介词短语

• The swimming pool is **on your right**.

游泳池在你的右边。

表示方式的介词短语

• She was famous **as a writer**.

她作为作家名气很大。

3 用作表语的介词短语要放在系动词之后。

介词短语 on the desk 作表语

• The keys you are looking for are **on the desk**.

你找的钥匙在书桌上。

介词短语 out of stock 作表语

• The red car is **out of stock**.

这款红色的车已经脱销了。

4 用作定语的介词短语只能放在被修饰的名词之后。

with a beautiful view 修饰名词 a city

• A city **with a beautiful view** is attractive.

一座拥有美丽风景的城市是很吸引人的。

from Britain 用来修饰名词 the girl

• The girl **from Britain** has golden hair.

这个来自英国的女孩有一头金发。

介词短语的作用

1 充当主语

• **Over 30 yuan** was spent on the pen.

这支笔花了 30 多元。

• **From Beijing to London** is a long distance.

从北京到伦敦是一段很长的路程。

2 充当补语

• Don't leave your toys **all over the floor**.

不要把你的玩具扔得满地都是。

• I saw you **in a white dress** today.

我看见你今天穿着一条白色连衣裙。

3 充当表语

• My home is **next to the school**.

我家就在学校旁边。

• Many high-quality products are **from China**.

许多高质量的产品都来自中国。

4 充当定语

- The girl **next to you** is my girlfriend.
  你旁边的那个女孩是我的女朋友。
- She devotes herself to helping people **in need**.
  她致力于帮助有需要的人。

5 充当状语

表原因

- **Thanks to** your advice, I saved my legs.
  多亏了你的建议，我保住了双腿。

表时间

- My father goes to work **from Monday to Friday**.
  我父亲从周一到周五去上班。

Exercise

根据图片在空格处填上合适的介词，补全句子。

1. They had a good time _____ the beach.

2. There are many clouds _____ the sky.

3. A stream is _____ my house.

4. I put the keys _____ the table.

5. Many people choose to go to work _____ underground.

6. I often draw _____ a pencil.

参考答案：

1. on　2. in　3. before　4. on　5. by　6. with

71

第三单元 常用介词辨析

through, across

through 表示"从……内部穿过"，比如人群、树林、门洞等。

- I walked **through** the forest before dark.
  天黑前我穿过了森林。

across 表示"从……表面穿过"，比如乘船过江或过河。

- I can swim **across** the river.
  我能游过这条河。

between, among

between 表示"两者之间"，常和 **and** 连用构成 **between ... and ...**。

- He slung a hammock **between** the two trees.
  他在两棵树之间挂了一个吊床。

among 表示在"在三者或三者以上之间"。

- Bees buzzed **among** the flowers.
  蜜蜂在花丛中嗡嗡作响。

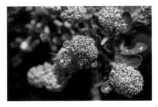

in, on, to 表示"位于"

in 表示在某一地区内的某方位，属于该范围。

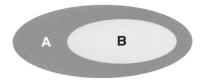

B is **in** the east of A

on 表示两地点相邻、接壤。

B is **on** the east of A

to 表示在某一地区之外的某方位，不属于该范围。

B is **to** the east of A

地点介词 at，in，on

at 表示某个具体的地点，着重指场所。
at home 在家   at airport 在机场

in 指的是某个地点范围，尤其指一些大的地点，如国家，城市等。
in America 在美国   in Paris 在巴黎

on 表示在某个平面上。
on the beach 在海滩上

地点介词 above，over

above 指的是在上方，表示相对高度。其反义词是 **below**。

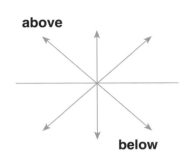

over 指的是正上方，其反义词是 **under**。

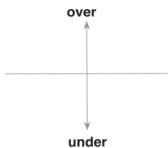

- The booms landed **above** the roof tops, and many people got injured.
  炸弹落在房顶上，炸伤了很多人。
- Please don't write words **below** the lines.
  请不要在线下面写字。

- The enemy planes circled **over** the mountains.
  敌军的飞机在山上盘旋。
- In order to avoid the war, the people have to hide **under** the bomb shelters.
  为了躲避战火，人们只能躲在防空洞下。

 **Exercise**

为下列句子勾选正确的答案。

1. The soldier fled ○ **through** ○ **across** the border.

2. The naughty boy climbed ○ **through** ○ **across** the window.

3. I need to choose ○ **between** ○ **among** the two jobs.

4. They divided the toys up ○ **between** ○ **among** the children.

5. How long will you stay ○ **at** ○ **in** London?

6. I seem to have left my wallet ○ **at** ○ **in** home.

7. Tibet lies ○ **to** ○ **in** the west of China.

8. Korea lies ○ **on** ○ **to** the east of China.

9. China lies ○ **in** ○ **to** the north of Vietnam.

参考答案：
1. across   2. through   3. between   4. among   5. in   6. at   7. in   8. on   9. to

第四单元 常用介词短语一览

介词 + 名词

at	
at peace 处于和平中	
at present 目前	
at rest 静止	
at sea 茫然	
at the moment 此时	
at times 有时	
at work 在工作	
at noon 在中午	

out of	
out of breath 喘不过气来	
out of control 不受控制	
out of date 过时	
out of fashion 不流行	
out of order 出故障	
out of work 失业	
out of place 不在合适的位置	
out of shape 走样，不成形	
out of the question 不可能	
out of question 毫无疑问	

in	
in comfort 舒适地	
in a moment 立即，马上	
in danger 在危险中	
in surprise 吃惊地	
in anger 生气地	
in excitement 激动地	

with	
with care 小心地	
with confidence 有信心地	
with courage 勇敢地	
with joy 高兴地	
with pleasure 愉快地	
with pride 骄傲地	

under	
under control 处于控制之下	
under pressure 在压力下	
under repair 在修理中	
under treatment 在治疗中	

on	
on holiday 度假	
on account of 因为	
on business 出差	
on fire 着火	
on display 展览	
on sale 出售，打折	

be + 形容词 + 介词

about	
be careful about 小心……	be excited about 对……感到兴奋
be happy about 对……感到开心	be serious about 对……认真
be sorry about 对……感到抱歉	be sure about 对……有把握
be worried about 对……担心	

at
be bad at 不擅长
be angry at 对……发怒
be good at 擅长

in
be dressed in 穿着……
be rich in 富有……
be skilled in 精通
be weak in 不擅长
be interested in 对……感兴趣

from
be absent from 缺席
be different from 不同于
be far from 远离
be free from 免于
be safe from 免受……的伤害

for
be famous for 以……著名
be fit for 适合，胜任
be good for 对……有益
be late for 迟到
be ready for 准备好……

to	of	with
be close to 接近	be afraid of 害怕	be busy with 忙于
be good to 对……好	be fond of 喜欢	be angry with 生气
be thankful to 感激	be short of 短缺	be filled with 充满
be friendly to 对……友好	be tired of 厌烦	be pleased with 满意
be rude to 对……无礼	be proud of 自豪	be connected with 与……有关
be similar to 与……相似	be sure of 坚信	be patient with 对……耐心
be useful to 对……有用	be full of 充满	be popular with 受……欢迎
be polite to 对……礼貌	be worthy of 值得	be satisfied with 对……满意

 **Exercise**

一、在空格处填上合适的介词，补全句子。

1. The machine is _____ of order.

2. She is good _____ oral English.

3. The situation is _____ control.

4. I am worried _____ losing my job.

5. It was not a pleasant ride because the city was full _____ people.

二、为下列句子勾选正确的答案。

1. The goods in the supermarket are ○ **on** ○ **in** sale.

2. Out ○ **from** ○ **of** question, it is her handwriting.

3. I am angry ○ **at** ○ **in** your attitude.

4. Tom used to be weak ○ **at** ○ **in** English.

5. I get up early in order not to be late ○ **for** ○ **to** work.

参考答案：
一、1. out   2. at   3. under/out of   4. about   5. of
二、1. on   2. of   3. at   4. in   5. for

第六章

形容词和副词
Adjectives and Adverbs

第一单元 形容词的构成

1 加后缀组成的形容词

构成方式	形容词
名词加 y	fun—funny 有趣的；sun—sunny 晴朗的 wind—windy 多风的
加后缀 able	admire—admirable 令人钦佩的；advise—advisable 可取的；明智的 comfort—comfortable 令人舒适的
加后缀 al	nation—national 国家的；nature—natural 天然的 person—personal 个人的
加后缀 en	wood—wooden 木制的；wool—woolen 羊毛的
加后缀 ern	east—eastern 东方的；west—western 西方的 south—southern 南方的；north—northern 北方的
加后缀 ent	differ—different 不同的；insist—insistent 坚持的
加后缀 ish	child—childish 孩子气的；self—selfish 自私的
加后缀 ive	act—active 积极的；expense—expensive 昂贵的 impress—impressive 印象深刻的
加后缀 ful	beauty—beautiful 漂亮的；faith—faithful 忠诚的 help—helpful 有帮助的；peace—peaceful 和平的 power—powerful 有影响力的；thank—thankful 感谢的 use—useful 有用的
加后缀 ous	danger—dangerous 有危险的；envy—envious 羡慕的，忌妒的 fame—famous 著名的
名词加 ly	cost—costly 昂贵的；day—daily 每天的 father—fatherly 慈父般的；man—manly 有男子汉气概的 month—monthly 每月的；order—orderly 有秩序的 time—timely 及时的；year—yearly 每年的

2 复合形容词的构成

副词 + 现在分词

ever-lasting 永恒的

hard-working 勤劳的

far-reaching 影响深远的

副词 + 过去分词

low-paid 低收入的

well-known 众所周知的

so-called 所谓的

名词 + 现在分词

life-saving 求生的

peace-loving 爱好和平的

English-speaking 讲英语的

名词 + 形容词

duty-free 免税的

ice-cold 冰冷的

life-long 终生的

名词 + 过去分词

man-made 人造的

snow-covered 被雪覆盖的

hand-made 手工制造的

heart-broken 心碎的

形容词 + 现在分词

easy-going 悠闲的

good-looking 好看的

ordinary-looking 长相一般的

long-suffering 长期忍受的

形容词 + 名词 ed

kind-hearted 好心的

absent-minded 心不在焉的

good-natured 脾气好的

形容词 + 过去分词

ready-made 现成的

new-born 新生的

full-grown 发育完全的

数词 + 名词

five-star 五星级的

four-year-old 四岁的

形容词 + 形容词

bitter-sweet 悲喜交加的

dark-green 深绿色的

3 很多动词的现在分词和过去分词都可作形容词使用。一般来说，现在分词转化来的形容词表示主动意义，用来修饰物。过去分词转化来的形容词则表示被动意义，常用来修饰人。

{ amazing 令人惊愕的
  amazed 惊讶的

{ exciting 令人激动的
  excited 激动的

{ interesting 令人感兴趣的
  interested 感兴趣的

{ surprising 使人惊奇的
  surprised 吃惊的

第二单元 形容词的位置

1 形容词作定语一般位于被修饰的名词之前，但 **asleep，awake，alive** 作定语时，常放在被修饰词的后面。

a **lovely** girl 一个可爱的女孩

interesting movies 有趣的电影

• Mary was the only girl **asleep** at the time.
玛丽是当时唯一睡着的女孩。

2 形容词修饰 **something，anything** 等不定代词时，要放在不定代词的后面。**enough** 修饰形容词时，放在形容词后面。

• John is very busy because he has **something important** to do.
约翰很忙，因为他有重要的事情要做。

• There is **nothing interesting** in the film.
这个电影毫无趣味。

• It is not **interesting enough** for me to work as a cashier.
当收银员对我来说不够有趣。

> **enough** 修饰名词时，既可放在名词的前面，也可放在名词的后面。

3 表语形容词用来说明主语的性质、特征、状态等，在句子中必须和系动词一起构成复合谓语。表语只能放在系动词之后，不能放在名词前作定语。

afraid	alone	asleep
awake	ill	well
ready	unable	sorry

（ × ）She is a **ill** girl.

（ √ ）She is **ill**.
她生病了。

4 有时一个名词由很多形容词共同修饰，有一定的排序规则：

限定词（冠词、指示代词、物主代词、数词等）+ 表示观点的描述性形容词（即表示好、坏、美、丑等）+ 大小、长短、高低 + 形状 + 年龄、新旧 + 颜色 + 国籍、地区 + 物质材料 + 名词

a big round red apple 一个又大又圆的红苹果

（冠词 + 大小 + 形状 + 颜色 + 名词）

an old black woolen carpet 一块旧的黑色羊毛地毯

（冠词 + 新旧 + 颜色 + 物质材料 + 名词）

一、将下列单词按照正确的顺序排序。

1. a   such   long   dress   white   pretty

_____

2. second   desk   the   red   long   wooden

_____

3. hair   short   brown   her   curly   beautiful

_____

4. English   two   another   novels

_____

5. the   short   men   old   Chinese   both

_____

二、将下面错误的句子改写正确。

1. She wears a woolen white shirt. _____

2. I am the only awake person in the room. _____

3. I bought a little fine doll. _____

4. The red beautiful wallet has been sold out. _____

5. This is the first beautiful iron Chinese bridge. _____

参考答案：

一、1. such a pretty long white dress   2. the second long red wooden desk
　　3. her beautiful short curly brown hair   4. another two English novels
　　5. both the short old Chinese men
二、1. She wears a white woolen shirt.   2. I am the only person awake in the room.
　　3. I bought a fine little doll.   4. The beautiful red wallet has been sold out.
　　5. This is the first beautiful Chinese iron bridge.

第三单元 副词的构成

1 简单副词

fast 快速地	there 那里
enough 足够地	very 非常
here 这里	quite 相当
rather 相当	now 现在
then 那时	

有些以 ly 结尾的词是形容词而不是副词。 如：lovely，lively，friendly，lonely，motherly 等。

2 与形容词形式相同的副词

单词	形容词词义	副词词义
early	提早的	提早
enough	足够的	足够地
fast	快的	快
hard	硬的	努力地
late	晚的	晚
long	长的	长期地
straight	直的	径直
very	正是的	非常，很

3 由形容词加 ly 构成的副词

情况	构成	示例
一般情况	加 -ly	brave—bravely 勇敢地 quick—quickly 迅速地 immediate—immediately 立即
双音节、多音节，以 y 结尾	将 y 改成 i 再加 -ly	busy—busily 忙碌地 easy—easily 容易地 happy—happily 高兴地
以 le 结尾	去 e 加 -y	comfortable—comfortably 舒服地 possible—possibly 可能地 simple—simply 仅仅
以元音字母加 e 结尾	去 e 加 -ly	true—truly 真实地
以 ll 结尾	只加 -y	dull—dully 迟钝地 full—fully 完全地
以 ic 结尾	加 -ally	basic—basically 基本上 scientific—scientifically 合乎科学地

4 有两种形式的副词

形容词	副词和形容词同形	形容词加 ly 的副词
close 近的，亲密的	close 接近（指距离）	closely 密切地，仔细地
dead 死的	dead 完全地	deadly 非常
deep 深的	deep 在深处	deeply 深刻地，深沉地
fair 公正的	fair 公正地	fairly 相当地
hard 坚硬的	hard 努力；猛烈地	hardly 几乎不
just 公正的	just 恰好，只是	justly 公正地
late 迟到的，晚的	late 迟，晚	lately 最近
near 近的	near 接近	nearly 几乎
wide 宽阔的	wide 充分地	widely 广泛地

有些副词是由介词或地点名词加后缀 ward(s) 构 成 的，意为"向……"。如：backward(s), downward(s), forward(s), northward(s), onward(s)。

Exercise

将下面单词按要求分类。

> **costly   well-known   certainly   quickly   manly   simply   lovely**
> **happily   totally   natural**

形容词	副词

参考答案：

形容词：costly   well-known   manly   lovely   natural

副词：certainly   quickly   simply   happily   totally

第四单元 副词的分类

按意义分类

1 表示时间的副词。

yesterday 昨天	today 今天
later 后来	before 之前
ever 曾经	now 现在
lately 最近	ago 以前
soon 很快	

2 表示频率的副词。

never 从不	usually 通常
often 经常	always 总是
sometimes 有时	frequently 频繁地
once 一次	twice 两次
seldom 很少	

3 表示地点、方向的副词。

in 在里面	inside 在里面
out 在外面	outside 在外面
upstairs 在楼上	downstairs 在楼下
below 在下面	above 在上面
everywhere 到处	anywhere 在任何地方
across 在对面	somewhere 在某处

4 表示方式的副词。

gently 温柔地	angrily 生气地
politely 有礼貌地	happily 高兴地
sincerely 真诚地	calmly 冷静地
slowly 缓慢地	suddenly 突然地
directly 直接地	

5 表示程度的副词。

much 非常	very 非常
extremely 非常	utterly 完全地
entirely 完全地	totally 完全地
quite 相当	rather 相当
pretty 相当	almost 几乎
hardly 几乎不	simply 仅仅
so 如此	still 仍然
enough 足够地	

> 这些词一般位于所修饰的词之前。

按功能分类

1 疑问副词。

when 什么时候	where 哪里
why 为什么	how 如何

2 解释副词（包括词组）。

namely 也就是	for example 比如
for instance 例如	

3 连接副词。

表示转折：however 然而，nevertheless 然而，nonetheless 尽管如此，though 虽然

表示条件：otherwise 否则

表示结果：consequently 因此，so 因此，therefore 因此

表示时间：before 以前，later 以后，next 接下来，then 然后

表示递进：furthermore 此外，moreover 此外

Exercise

结合图片，用括号中所给词的正确形式填空。

1. I haven't been sleeping well
   _____. (late)

2. How _____ (happy) these children
   are playing!

3. I put on my coat and went out
   _____. (quick)

4. Tina _____ (grateful) received
   the presents from her friends.

5. I was pleased to know that you
   arrived home _____. (safe)

6. The door was _____ (sudden)
   open.

7. She held the baby _____ (gentle)
   in her arms.

8. He _____ (frequent) donates
   money to charity.

9. The problem can be handled
   _____ (easy) for me.

10. My house is _____ (simple)
    furnished.

参考答案：

1. lately 2. happily 3. quickly 4. gratefully 5. safely 6. suddenly

7. gently 8. frequently 9. easily 10. simply

第五单元 形容词/副词比较级和最高级的变化

规则变化

单音节形容词和副词 + -er/-est

warm → warmer → warmest

small → smaller → smallest

hard → harder → hardest

quick → quicker → quickest

以 e 结尾的单音节形容词和副词 + -r/-st

wide → wider → widest

rude → ruder → rudest

多音节副词和以 ly 结尾的副词，都在原级前 + more/most（early 除外）

intelligently → more intelligently → most intelligently

successfully → more successfully → most successfully

以重读闭音节结尾的形容词的最后一个辅音字母要双写，然后再 + -er/-est

thin → thinner → thinnest

hot → hotter → hottest

wet → wetter → wettest

big → bigger → biggest

以"辅音字母 + y"结尾的双音节形容词，要把 y 变为 i，再 + -er/-est

happy → happier → happiest

lucky → luckier → luckiest

early → earlier → earliest

ready → readier → readiest

以 er, ow 结尾的双音节形容词，直接在后面 + -er/-est

clever → cleverer → cleverest

bitter → bitterer → bitterest

slow → slower → slowest

narrow → narrower → narrowest

部分双音节和多音节形容词前面 + more/most

tired → more tired → most tired

beautiful → more beautiful → most beautiful

少数以"辅音字母 + y"结尾的形容词在变为比较级和最高级时，既可以在后面直接 + -er /-est，也可以在前面 + more/most。

common → commoner/more common → commonest/most common

simple → simpler/more simple → simplest/most simple

不规则变化

little → less → least

many/much → more → most

good/well → better → best

bad → worse → worst

old → older/elder → oldest/eldest

far → farther/further → farthest/furthest

没有比较级和最高级的情况

具有唯一性含义的词。

only 唯一的   sole 单独的   unique 独一无二的

具有完全性含义的词。

absolute 绝对的   full 满的   perfect 完美的

具有极端、主次性含义的词。

basic 基本的   extreme 极端的   primary 主要的

本身具有比较含义的词。

superior 上等的   inferior 下等的

表示"材料、性质、国籍"的词。

gold 金的   wrong 错的   Chinese 中国的，中国人的

表示"方位、时间"的词。

westward 向西的   upstairs 楼上的   weekly 每周的

Exercise

写出下列各词的比较级和最高级。

1. busy _____ _____   2. thin _____ _____

3. hot _____ _____   4. angry _____ _____

5. challenging _____ _____   6. wide _____ _____

7. few _____ _____   8. heavy _____ _____

9. beautiful _____ _____   10. narrow _____ _____

参考答案：

1. busier busiest   2. thinner thinnest   3. hotter hottest

4. angrier angriest   5. more challenging most challenging

6. wider widest   7. fewer fewest   8. heavier heaviest

9. more beautiful most beautiful   10. narrower narrowest

第六单元 形容词/副词比较级和最高级的一般用法

比较级

1 形容词和副词的比较级最常用的结构是 "**A + be 动词 + 比较级 + than + B**"，表示 "**A 比 B 更……**"。

- This tree is taller than that one.
  这棵树比那棵高。

- You made more mistakes than he did.
  你犯的错误比他多。

2 用 "**比较级 + and + 比较级**" 或 "**more and more + 原级**" 来表示 "**越来越……**"。

- The patient's condition is getting better and better.
  病人的情况越来越好了。

- The end of the novel is getting more and more exciting.
  小说的结尾越来越令人兴奋。

3 表示 "**越……越……**" 时的结构为 "**the + 比较级，the + 比较级**"。

- The more she gets, the more she wants.
  她得到的越多，想要的就越多。

- The more you speak, the better your oral Japanese will be.
  你说得越多，你的日语口语就会越好。

4 表示倍数的比较级的结构为 "**A + be 动词 + 倍数 + 比较级 + than + B**"。

- The rope is twice longer than that one.
  这根绳子比那根长两倍。

- My box is ten times heavier than yours.
  我的箱子比你的箱子重十倍。

平级比较的用法：
肯定句：as + 形容词原级 + as
Mary's oral English is as good as mine.
玛丽的英语口语和我的一样好。
否定句：not as/so ... as ...
My work is not as/so beautiful as hers.
我的作品不如她的漂亮。

最高级

最高级一般用于三者以上的比较，其结构为 "**A + 谓语动词 + the + 最高级（ + 其他成分）**"，有的副词最高级前可以省略 the。

- China is one of the largest countries in the world.
  中国是世界上最大的国家之一。

- Lily is the most beautiful girl in our class.
  莉莉是我们班最漂亮的女孩。

- She runs fastest among us.
  她在我们中跑得最快。
  （省略 the）

比较范围可以用短语、从句表示。
He is the cleverest of us.
他是我们当中最聪明的。
This is the most ridiculous movie I've ever seen.
这是我看过的最可笑的电影。

一、用括号中所给词的正确形式填空。

1. You look _____ (fat) than before.

2. Which is _____ (expensive), the red one or the yellow one?

3. I think Sally is the _____ (kind) person in the world.

4. This orange is a little _____ (big) than that one.

5. My room is not as _____ (clean) as my sister's.

6. Tina is _____ (beautiful) than her little sister.

7. Bob is the _____ (tall) boy in the class.

8. He is one of the _____ (friendly) people in the class.

9. I think physics is _____ (difficult) than math.

10. Monday is my _____ (busy) day in a week.

二、翻译下面句子。

1. It is a perfect day for a picnic.

_____

2. This room is twice bigger than that one.

_____

3. Your room is wider and brighter than mine.

_____

4. I think tiger is the most dangerous animal in the world.

_____

5. London is the biggest city in Britain.

_____

参考答案：
一、1. fatter   2. more expensive   3. kindest   4. bigger   5. clean
    6. more beautiful   7. tallest   8. friendliest   9. more difficult   10. busiest
二、1. 今天是野餐的好天气。   2. 这个房间比那个房间大两倍。
    3. 你的房间比我的更宽阔、明亮。   4. 我认为老虎是世界上最危险的动物。
    5. 伦敦是英国最大的城市。

第七单元 形容词/副词比较级和最高级的特殊用法

1 如果在两者的比较中有表示选择的含义，可以用"**A + be 动词 + the + 比较级 + of + B**"结构。

· The watch is the **better of the two**.
这个手表是两个之中比较好的。

2 **not ... any more than ...** 和 **no more ... than ...** 这两个结构虽然含有 **more than**，但是并没有比较含义。它们表示"和……一样都不……"。

· He may **not** like math **any more than** I do.

> 没有比较含义

= He may like **no more** math **than** I do.
他可能和我一样不喜欢数学。

3 比较级和最高级的修饰词

比较级： much even still yet by far
far and away a lot a great deal
a little a bit

最高级： much by far nearly almost
the very

4 比较级有时可单独使用，其比较的对象暗含于句中。

> 和之前的工作进行比较

· I hope to get a **better** job.
我希望能找到一份更好的工作。

> 今天和昨天的状态进行比较

· I am feeling **better** today.
我今天感觉好多了。

5 "最……"的其他表示法。

◉ 比较级 + than any other ...

· Julia is shorter **than any other** girl in her family.
= Julia is **the shortest** girl in her family.
茱莉亚比她家里的任何其他女孩都矮。

· Jim does his homework more carefully **than any other** boy in his class.
= Jim is the boy who does his homework **most carefully** in the class.
吉姆做作业比班上任何其他男孩都认真。

◉ ... never ... + 比较级 /not ... ever ... + 比较级

· I've **never** heard a better voice than hers.
= Her voice is **the best** that I've ever heard.
我从来没听过比她更好的嗓音。

· I do**n't** think I have **ever** been happier in my life.
= This is **the happiest** time in my life.
我觉得我这辈子从来没有这么快乐过。

◉ nothing/nobody ... + 比较级 + than ...

· **Nothing** is **more** important **than** to receive good education.
= Receiving good education is **the most** important thing.
没有比接受良好的教育更重要的事。

 **Exercise**

一、根据句意，完成下列句子。

1. 杰克的母亲比父亲大三岁。

   Jack's mother is _____ _____ _____ than his father.

2. 我对跳舞越来越感兴趣了。

   I became _____ _____ _____ interested in dancing.

3. 在我看来，这部电影不如那部有趣。

   In my opinion, the film is _____ _____ _____ as that one.

4. 地球是月球的 49 倍。

   The Earth is _____ _____ _____ _____ _____ the moon.

5. 我和朱迪一样不喜欢摇滚。

   I don't like rock _____ _____ _____ Judy does.

6. 越来越多的孩子沉迷于电脑游戏。

   _____ _____ _____ children are addicted to computer games.

7. 你开始得越早，完成得就越快。

   The _____ you start, the _____ you will finish.

8. 他不是学者，正如我不是作家一样。

   He is not a scholar _____ _____ _____ I am a writer.

二、为下列句子勾选正确的答案。

1. Annie is ○ **much** ○ **more** taller than me.

2. I think she is the ○ **friendlier** ○ **friendliest** teacher in the school.

3. He is as ○ **strong** ○ **stronger** as ever.

4. This notebook is much ○ **more expensive** ○ **most expensive** than that one.

5. The Changjiang river is the ○ **longer** ○ **longest** river in China.

参考答案：

一、1. three years older   2. more and more   3. not as/so interesting

  4. forty-nine times the size of   5. any more than   6. More and more

  7. earlier; faster   8. any more than

二、1. much   2. friendliest   3. strong   4. more expensive   5. longest

第七章

连词
Conjunctions

第一单元 并列连词

and

and 可用来连接两个或两个以上的单词、短语或句子，表示一种对等或顺承关系。

- Sheila **and** I both like carrots.

  希拉和我都喜欢胡萝卜。

- My brother is playing basketball **and** my sister is watching TV.

  我弟弟在打篮球，我妹妹在看电视。

- She felt dizzy **and** then passed out.

  她感到头晕，然后就晕过去了。

both ... and ...

both ... and ... 意为 "……和……都"，用来连接两个并列的主语、谓语、宾语、表语和状语等。连接两个并列的主语时，谓语动词用复数形式。

- I can play **both** the piano **and** erhu.

  我既会弹钢琴又会拉二胡。

- **Both** Lily **and** Mike **are** good at playing table tennis.

  莉莉和迈克都擅长打乒乓球。

neither ... nor ...

neither ... nor ... 意为 "既不……也不……"，连接两个主语、谓语、宾语、表语和状语等。

- Professor Zhang spoke **neither** Japanese **nor** French.

  张教授既不会说日语也不会说法语。

- **Neither** Jim **nor** I have heard this news.

  吉姆和我都没有听到这个消息。

not only ... but (also) ...

not only ... but (also) ... 意为 "不但……而且……"，可连接两个主语、谓语、宾语、表语和状语，也可连接句子。

- He **not only** won **but also** made history in the competition.

  他不仅赢得了比赛，而且创造了历史。

- **Not only** Jane **but** her parents are kind to me.

  不仅简就连她的父母都对我很好。

一、从下面四个选项中选出最佳答案。

1. I went to the bookstore _____ bought some books.
   A. and   B. but   C. so   D. or

2. Study hard, _____ you will get good grades.
   A. or   B. however   C. so   D. and

3. She not only studies well, _____ also plays sports well.
   A. so   B. but   C. or   D. and

4. I neither knew _____ cared what was wrong with her.
   A. and   B. but   C. nor   D. so

5. _____ Mike and Tina are members of the student union.
   A. Both   B. Not only   C. Neither   D. And

二、判断下面的句子是否使用了并列连词。是的在句子的后面打"√"，不是的打"×"。

1. They sat down and talked about the new film. （　）

2. Some people like animals while others don't like them. （　）

3. I want to go to the college but my parents want me to work. （　）

4. I am so hungry and then I order some food. （　）

5. Both Tina and Judy like to play games. （　）

6. I am both a good swimmer and a good cook. （　）

7. He hasn't finished his homework yet. （　）

8. My mother won't let me go out unless I have someone with me. （　）

9. Steve is tall and thin and has black hair. （　）

10. However, she underestimated the seriousness of the problem. （　）

参考答案：
一、1. A　2. D　3. B　4. C　5. A
二、1. √　2. ×　3. ×　4. √　5. √　6. √　7. ×　8. ×　9. √　10. ×

第二单元 转折连词

but

but 意为"但是、然而、可是"。注意：**although** 不能和 **but** 同时用。

- She is not rich, **but** she is happy.

  她不富有，但她很快乐。

- He is silly, **but** he has a good heart.

  他很傻，但有一颗善良的心。

yet

yet 意为"但是、然而"，表示惊讶或者转折。

- It's a small room, **yet** it's very clean.

  这个房间很小，但是很干净。

- It's warm, **yet** he wears a lot.

  天气暖和，但他穿得很多。

while

while 意为"然而"，在表示转折关系时，往往连接内容和结构对称的两部分，常用来表示鲜明的对比。

- I like milk **while** my mother likes coffee.

  我喜欢牛奶，然而我妈妈喜欢咖啡。

- She played tennis **while** the others went swimming.

  她去打网球，而其他人去游泳了。

however

however 表示转折，用在句中时要用逗号将前后句子隔开。

- It's time to have dinner, **however**, she hasn't been back home.

  该吃晚餐了，然而，她还没有回家。

- He fell asleep, **however**, the light was still on.

  他睡着了，但灯还开着。

 **Exercise**

一、将下面错误的句子改写正确。

1. I know her face so I can't remember her name. _____

2. My mother bought not snacks and vegetables for me. _____

3. Although potato chips are delicious, but don't eat too much. _____

4. I like apples so Judy likes oranges. _____

5. She was ill, but, she persisted in going to work. _____

二、从下面四个选项中选出最佳答案。

1. The snow stopped, _____ it's getting colder.
   A. yet   B. and   C. so   D. or

2. My father is cooking _____ my mother is sleeping.
   A. but   B. yet   C. while   D. or

3. _____, everything has two sides.
   A. But   B. However   C. While   D. Yet

4. She is not ugly, _____ behaves strangely.
   A. but   B. and   C. so   D. or

5. Tina was seriously ill, _____ she still attended the meeting.
   A. but   B. and   C. so   D. or

参考答案：

一、1. I know her face but I can't remember her name.

　　2. My mother bought not snacks but vegetables for me/My mother bought both snacks and vegetables for me.

　　3. Although potato chips are delicious, don't eat too much./Potato chips are delicious, but don't eat too much.

　　4. I like apples while Judy likes oranges.

　　5. She was ill, however, she persisted in going to work.

二、1. A　2. C　3. B　4. A　5. A

第三单元 选择连词和因果连词

选择连词

1 or

　　or 意为"或者，否则"，表示"否则"时，前面的句子一般是祈使句，后面的句子通常要用一般将来时。or 还常用在否定句或疑问句中表示并列，相当于 and。

- It may be black or white.
  它可能是黑色或白色的。

- Hurry up, or we will be late.
  快点，否则我们就要迟到了。

- Would you like wine or champagne?
  你想喝葡萄酒还是香槟？

2 either ... or ...

　　either ... or ... 意为"或者……或者……，不是……就是……，要么……要么……"。如果连接两个并列主语，谓语动词与 or 后的主语保持一致。

- I am going to buy either a piano or a guitar.
  我要么买一架钢琴，要么买一把吉他。

- Either he or you are right.
  不是他对就是你对。

3 not ... but ...

　　not ... but ... 意为"不是……而是……"。

- She is not a doctor but a lawyer.
  她不是一位医生而是一名律师。

因果连词

1 so

　　so 意为"所以、因此"，后面接的句子表结果。

- I got ill so I took medicine.
  我生病了，所以我吃了药。

- It was dark, so he went home.
  天黑了，所以他回家了。

2 for

　　for 意为"因为、由于"，后面的分句通常表示一种推断性的原因，是对前一分句的补充。此时 for 连接的分句不能放在句首。

- It must have rained last night, for the ground is wet all over.
  昨天晚上一定下雨了，因为地面上到处都是湿的。

for 和 because 的区别
for 连接的分句只能放在句尾，前面用逗号隔开，表示补充说明或者提供推断的理由。
because 表示的是一种明确的因果关系，解释原因，既可以位于主句前也可位于主句后，常回答 why 引导的问句。

 **Exercise**

一、从下面四个选项中选出最佳答案。

1. _____ my father _____ my mother is at home today. They are on business.

　　A. Neither; nor　　　　B. Both; and　　　　C. Either; or　　　　D. Not; but

2. You can sit on _____ this end _____ that end of the bench.

　　A. neither; or　　　　B. both; and　　　　C. either; or　　　　D. no; but

3. We went _____ to the cinema _____ to the park. We had a great time.

　　A. neither; nor　　　　B. not; and　　　　C. either; or　　　　D. not only; but also

4. She is _____ ill _____ tired. She needs a break.

　　A. neither; nor　　　　B. both; and　　　　C. either; or　　　　D. not; but

5. — Why are you so sad?

　　— _____ I failed the interview.

　　A. So　　　　　　　　B. Because　　　　C. For　　　　　　D. But

二、在空格处填上合适的连词，补全句子。

1. Hurry up, _____ we will be late for the work.

2. Both my father _____ brother are doctors.

3. The teacher looks tired, _____ he sat up all day.

4. He must be at home, _____ the light in his room is on.

5. I am praised _____ I work so hard.

6. She must be either drunk _____ mad.

7. The fruit are not just for you _____ for everyone.

8. _____ Mary but also Tom is fond of watching television.

参考答案：

一、1. A　2. C　3. D　4. D　5. B

二、1. or　2. and　3. because　4. for　5. because　6. or　7. but　8. Not only

第四单元 常用连词辨析

1 because 和 so；although/though 和 but 不能同时出现在一个句子中。

- They put off the match, **because** it rained heavily.

  = It rained heavily, **so** they put off the match.

  他们推迟了比赛，因为雨下得很大。

  (×) Because it rained heavily, so they put off the match.

- **Though** she was tired, she still studied harder.

  = She was tired, **but** she still studied harder.

  虽然她累了，但她仍然更加努力地学习。

  (×) Though she was tired, but she still studied harder.

2 if 的两种意思

if { 意为"是否"，引导宾语从句，同 whether。
     意为"假如，如果"，引导条件状语从句。

if 意为"是否"，引导宾语从句

- We don't know **if** the weather will be fine tomorrow.

  我们不知道明天天气好不好。

if 意为"如果"，引导时间状语从句

- **If** the weather is fine tomorrow, I will go shopping with you.

  如果明天天气好，我就和你一起去购物。

3 until 和 before

until 表示"直到……才"，用于肯定句中，主句的动词为延续性动词；用于否定句中，主句的动词为非延续性动词，此时与 before 同义。before 表示"在……之前"，强调时间先后关系。

- I **lay** sleepless **until** dawn.

  我躺在那儿，直到天亮才睡着。

- She will not **come** back **until/before** it is dark. 她直到天黑才回来。

- I often run **before** going to work.

  我常常在上班前跑步。

4 as, as soon as, when, while

as 表示"当……时；随着"，常用来指瞬间动作或事件同时发生。as soon as 表示"一……就……"，指两个相继发生的动作。when 表示两个动作先后发生或同时进行，它可以指某一时间点，也可以表示一段时间。while 表示两个动作同时进行，不能表示某一时间点。常用来表示两个动作的对比。

- I saw her **as** she got off the train.

  当她下火车时，我看见了她。

- **As soon as** he got home, the doorbell rang. 他一到家，门铃就响了。

- I was listening to music **when** she came into my room.

  她走进我房间时，我正在听音乐。

- He fell asleep **while** he was doing his exercises. 他在做练习的时候睡着了。

Exercise

一、为下列句子勾选正确的答案。

1. Although the house is small, ○ / ○ **but** it is well designed.

2. I will help you ○ **if** ○ **whether** you are in trouble.

3. She was always trying out new ideas ○ **while** ○ **when** she was a child.

4. I was doing my homework ○ **while** ○ **when** my little sister was sleeping.

5. We got to the station ○ **until** ○ **before** it started to rain.

二、翻译下面句子。

1. 运动会被推迟了，因为天气不好。

_____

2. 我一遇到他就会告诉他这个消息。

_____

3. 如果明天不下雨，我们就去公园。

_____

4. 他们在唱歌，而我们在跳舞。

_____

5. 对不起，你打电话给我时我正忙于工作。

_____

参考答案：
一、1. /   2. if   3. when   4. while   5. before
二、1. The sports meeting was delayed, because the weather was terrible.

  2. I will tell him the news as soon as I meet him.

  3. If it doesn't rain tomorrow, we will go to the park.

  4. They are singing while we are dancing.

  5. Sorry, I was busy with work when you called me.

第八章

动词
Verbs

第一单元 动词的三种形态

动词的三种形态指的是动词的原形、过去式、过去分词。动词原形在变过去式和过去分词时有规则变化和不规则变化两种情况。

① 动词的规则变化（此时过去式和过去分词形式一致）

动词原形的结尾情况	过去式和过去分词	示例
一般情况	在结尾加 -ed	work → worked → worked
以 y 结尾，且 y 前面是辅音	把 y 变为 i，再加 -ed	try → tried → tried
以重读闭音节结尾	双写结尾的辅音字母，再加 -ed	plan → planned → planned
结尾是不发音的字母 e	在结尾加 -d	live → lived → lived
以 r 且是重读音节结尾	要双写 r 再加 -ed	stir → stirred → stirred

② 动词的不规则变化

动词的原形、过去式和过去分词都一样

cost → cost → cost 花费
cut → cut → cut 切，割
hurt → hurt → hurt 伤害
let → let → let 让
put → put → put 放
read → read → read 阅读
shut → shut → shut 关闭
hit → hit → hit 打，击
cast → cast → cast 投
bid → bid → bid 出价

动词的原形和过去分词一样，而过去式不同

become → became → become 变成，变得
come → came → come 来；来到
overcome → overcame → overcome 克服
run → ran → run 跑步

动词的过去式和过去分词相同

bring → brought → brought 带来；引起
catch → caught → caught 抓住；赶上
dig → dug → dug 挖，掘
feel → felt → felt 感受到；触摸
find → found → found 发现；找到
fight → fought → fought 打架
have → had → had 有；吃，喝
get → got → got 得到；到达
lend → lent → lent 借给
make → made → made 使；制作
meet → met → met 遇见
pay → paid → paid 支付
say → said → said 说，讲
sell → sold → sold 卖，出售
shine → shone → shone 发光，照耀
smell → smelt → smelt 嗅，闻
sit → sat → sat 坐
tell → told → told 告诉，讲述

动词的原形、过去式和过去分词均不相同

begin → began → begun 开始

blow → blew → blown 吹，刮

break → broke → broken 打破，打坏

choose → chose → chosen 选择

do → did → done 做，干

drink → drank → drunk 喝

eat → ate → eaten 吃

fall → fell → fallen 降落，落下

forget → forgot → forgotten 忘记

give → gave → given 送给，给予

go → went → gone 去，离去

lie → lay → lain 躺

rise → rose → risen 上升，上涨

see → saw → seen 看见；明白

sing → sang → sung 唱歌

speak → spoke → spoken 讲话，说话

swim → swam → swum 游泳

take → took → taken 拿，花费

wake → woke → woken 叫醒，醒来

write → wrote → written 书写，写作

Exercise

结合图片和首字母，将下面的单词补充完整，并用其正确形式。

1. I w_____ as a doctor in a big hospital last year.
   去年我在一家大医院当医生。

2. We h_____ a big welcome party for him yesterday.
   我们昨天为他举办了盛大的欢迎会。

3. We get p_____ at the end of the month.
   我们月底发工资。

4. W_____ up. It's time to get up.
   醒醒，该起床了。

参考答案：

1. worked 2. held 4. paid 5. Wake

第二单元 动词搭配

动词 + 介词

agree with 同意
I tend to agree with Tom.
我倾向于同意汤姆的看法。

ask for 请求
She was reluctant to ask for help.
她不愿意请求帮助。

carry on 坚持
If you carry on, you will succeed one day.
如果你坚持下去，总有一天会成功的。

knock at 敲门
It seems that someone is knocking at the door.
好像有人在敲门。

look after 照顾

It is our duty to look after the aged parents.
照顾年迈的父母是我们的责任。

look at 看
Look at that cat. It's so cute.
看那只猫，好可爱啊。

look down 看不起
They look down on outsiders.
他们看不起外来者。

look for 寻找
We are looking for simple solutions.
我们正在寻找简单的解决方法。

look like 看起来像
Your eyes look like stars. They're so beautiful.
你的眼睛像星星一样，好漂亮啊。

pay for 付钱

How would you like to pay for it?
你想如何付款？

stop ... from 阻止
We can't stop people from coming in.
我们不能阻止人们进来。

talk about 谈论，讨论
Don't talk about other people's family affairs.
不要谈论别人的家庭事务。

think of 认为，考虑
What do you think of this matter?
你对这件事怎么看？

regard ... as 把……当作
Don't regard the whole thing as a joke.
不要把整件事当作笑话。

动词 + 副词

come along 随同

I wish you could come along.

我希望你能一起来。

come out 出来，出版

Her new book has come out.

她的新书已经出版了。

come over 顺便来访

If you have time, please come over.

有空常来。

cut down 砍倒

The forest trees were cut down.

森林里的树被砍倒了。

fall behind 落后

Study hard, or you will fall behind.

努力学习，不然你就要落后了。

find out 找出

Police have not yet found out the murderer.

警察还没有找出凶手。

get down 下来

He yelled at the child to get down from the tree.

他喊着让孩子从树上下来。

work out 计算，解决

I can't work out this math problem.

我解不出这道数学题。

give away 泄露

Be careful not to give away your personal information.

小心不要泄露你的个人信息。

give up 放弃

Never give up easily.

不要轻易放弃。

go over 仔细检查

He would go over his work carefully.

他会仔细检查他的工作。

pick up 捡起；采摘

She bent down to pick up her wallet.

她俯身去捡钱包。

动词和副词搭配时，有时接人称代词作宾语。此时要将人称代词放在动词和副词之间，如 pick them up（把它们捡起来）。

slow down 减速

I get carsick, and you'd better slow down.

我晕车，你最好减速行驶。

take off 脱下，起飞

When will the plane take off?

飞机几点起飞？

turn off 关掉

Would you please turn off the TV?

请你把电视关掉好吗？

第三单元 使役动词

使役动词是表示"让/叫/使/帮/令"等意义的及物动词，而且是不完全的及物动词。

用法

1 have/make/let/help 作使役动词，后接动词原形，作宾语补足语。get 和 leave 作使役动词，其后接"to do 不定式"作宾语补足语。

> help 后用动词原形

- She helped me **get** the signature.

  她帮我拿到了签名。

> leave 后用动词不定式 to do

- Why don't you leave him **to try**?

  你何不让他自己尝试呢？

2 过去分词可以放在使役动词之后作宾语补足语。

> damaged 放在 had 后对宾语 house 补充说明

- He had his house **damaged** in the flood.

  他的房子在洪水中被毁了。

> cut 放在 have 后对宾语 hair 补充说明

- I would like to have my hair **cut**.

  我想剪头发。

3 使役动词的被动语态可以接"to do 不定式"作宾语补足语。

> to do 放在 leave 的被动形式 left 后

- I was left **to deal** with this matter on my own.

  就剩我一个人处理这件事。

> to do 放在 make 的被动形式 made 后

- Tina was made **to buy** soy sauce in the supermarket.

  蒂娜被叫去超市买酱油。

各个使役动词的用法

1 make

make 除了用于 make sb do sth 和 make sth done 句型外，还可用于 make sb sth，表示"为某人制作某物，让某人成为……"。

- Your behavior will **make me change** my mind.

  你的行为会让我改变主意的。

- She can hardly **make herself understood**.

  她很难使人明白她的意思。

- Studying hard can **make you a good person**.

  努力学习能让你成为一个优秀的人。

2 let

let 后直接加表示方向、方位的副词或介词。

- I won't **let you in** if you don't have the ticket.

  如果你没有票，我是不会让你进来的。

3 keep

keep 用于 keep sb/sth doing 和"keep sb/sth + 形容词/副词/介词（短语）"结构。

- I don't want to **keep you waiting** so long for me.

  我不想让你等我这么久。

- You must keep the room clean.

  你必须保持房间清洁。

4 have

have 可用于 have sth done，既可以表示"让 / 请别人做某事"，也可以表示"遭遇了某事"。

- They are going to **have some fruit trees planted**.

  他们打算种一些果树。

- I heard you **had your phone stolen**.

  我听说你的手机被偷了。

5 help

help 常用于 help sb with sth，表示"帮助某人做某事"。

- My deskmate **helps me with my study**.

  我的同桌帮助我学习。

6 leave

leave 既可用于 leave sb doing 的结构，表示"让某人继续处于某种状态"，也可用于"leave sb/sth + 形容词 / 介词短语"结构。

- The workers **leave the machine running**.

  工人让机器持续运转。

- Why don't you **leave me alone**?

  你能不能让我一个人待着？

Exercise

请勾选出正确的使役动词用法。

○ make you happy

○ let me to drive

○ keep you fit

○ have Tom punished

○ get it repairing

○ leave the door open

○ make her laughed

○ let you out

○ keep the girl standing

○ have her calling

○ help me with my homework

○ leave you wait

参考答案：

正确：make you happy　　let you out　　keep you fit　keep the girl standing

　　　have Tom punished　　help me with my homework　leave the door open

第四单元 及物动词和不及物动词

及物动词

及物动词是一种可以直接接宾语的动词，由于其不能表达完整的意义，需要接宾语才能使句子的意义更加完整。

接单宾语的及物动词		接双宾语的及物动词		接复合宾语的及物动词	
accept 接受	allow 允许	ask 要求	bring 带来	allow 允许	feel 感觉
begin 开始	bury 埋	hand 传递	lend 借	have 让	help 帮助
clean 清洁	eat 吃	offer 提供	send 送	find 发现	see 看见
forget 忘记	hurt 伤害	teach 教；讲授	write 写	tell 告诉	want 想要

不及物动词

不及物动词是一种不能直接接宾语的动词，其本身包含了完整的意义，一般构成"主语 + 谓语"的结构。

agree 同意	appear 出现	look 看	belong 属于	go 去
die 死	disagree 不同意	disappear 消失	exist 存在	listen 听

有些动词既可以作及物动词也可以作不及物动词，有的意义相同，有的不同。

意义相同的动词 { answer 回答　　close 关　　consider 考虑　hurt 伤害
　　　　　　　　 improve 改善　insist 坚持　learn 学习　prepare 准备

prepare 作及物动词，意为"准备"
· I have **prepared** all the materials. 我已经准备好了所有的材料。

prepare 作不及物动词，意为"准备"
· I have stepped up my training to **prepare** for the match. 我为准备那场比赛加强了训练。

意义不同的动词 { beat 敲打；跳动　　grow 种植；生长　operate 操作；动手术
　　　　　　　　 play 打球；玩耍　ring 打电话；铃响　　sell 卖；售价是……

play 作及物动词，意为"打球"
· The PE teacher teaches us to **play** basketball. 体育老师教我们打篮球。

play 作不及物动词，意为"玩耍"
· None of us wants to **play** with her. 我们都不想和她一起玩。

Exercise

一、根据句意补全句子，并将所填单词按要求进行分类。

1. I don't want to _____ the fact. 我不愿意接受这个事实。

2. I have a plan to _____ to the park. 我有一个去公园的计划。

3. We will _____ on his back. 我们要给他做背部手术。

4. My friends don't _____ with me. 我的朋友不同意我的观点。

5. I don't think this hero _____. 我认为这个英雄不存在。

6. Now the young don't _____ in marriage. 现在的年轻人不相信婚姻。

7. As the sun _____, the farmers begin to work. 太阳一出来，农民就开始工作了。

8. I finally _____ my keys. 我终于找到了我的钥匙。

9. I'll _____ you tomorrow. 我明天再给你打电话。

10. The supermarket _____ all kinds of things. 超市售卖各种各样的东西。

及物动词	不及物动词

二、找出下列句子的错误之处并改正。

1. The baby looks the toys all the time. _____

2. Do you believe the miracles exist in? _____

3. I like to play with soccer. _____

4. Tigers belong the cat family. _____

5. Do you want to listen music? _____

参考答案：

一、1. accept   2. go   3. operate   4. agree   5. exists
　　6. believe   7. appears   8. found   9. call   10. sells
　　及物动词：accept   found   call   sells
　　不及物动词：go   operate   agree   exists   believe   appears

二、1. looks 后加 at   2. 删去 in   3. 删去 with   4. belong 后加 to   5. listen 后加 to

第五单元 常见动词辨析

begin, start

begin 和 **start** 后接动名词或动词不定式时一般可以互相替换使用，但是 **start** 还有"启动，重新开始"的意思。

- I **began/started** to learn to play the piano at the age of ten.
  我十岁的时候开始学习弹钢琴。
- A new plan will be **started**.
  一个新的计划要启动了。

beat, win

beat 后一般接人，表示"打败某人"，**win** 后一般接比赛，表示"赢得比赛"。

- I don't think you can **beat** her.
  我觉得你赢不了她。
- I'm confident in **winning** the game.
  我有信心赢得这场比赛。

spend, take, cost, pay

1 **spend** 后一般接表示时间或金钱的名词，主语是人，用于句型"sb **spend** + 时间 / 金钱 + on sth/(in) doing sth"。

- I **spend** too much time (in) playing games.
  我花了太多的时间玩游戏。

2 **take** 的主语一般是物，但经常用形式主语 it 来代替真正的主语，用于句型"It/sth + **takes** + 时间 + to do sth"。

- It **took** me two hours to finish the project.
  我花了两小时完成这个项目。

3 **cost** 后一般接表示时间或金钱的名词，但与 **spend** 不同，**cost** 的主语一般是物。

- The ticket **cost** me 500 yuan.
  这张票花了我 500 元。

4 **pay** 后面的宾语是金钱，其结构为"sb + **pay** + 金钱 + for"。

- I **paid** four hundred dollars for this phone.
  我花了 400 美元买这部手机。

hope, wish

hope 表示实现的可能性比较大或者有较大的信心能够实现的"希望"，其后直接接动词不定式或者宾语从句。**wish** 表示实现的可能性不太大的"希望"，其后可以接名词、代词、动词不定式或从句。

- I **hope** to get home around two o'clock.
  我希望能在两点钟左右到家。
- She **wishes** it were not snowing now.
  她希望现在没有下雪。

bring, take, carry, lift, send

1 **bring** 指的是"拿来"。

- Waiter, can you **bring** me a glass of water?
  服务员，能给我一杯水吗？

2 **take** 指的是"带走"。
I'm going to **take** my computer upstairs.
我要把电脑拿到楼上去。

3 carry 指的是不含方向的"搬运，携带"。

· I always **carry** my backpack.

我总是携带着我的背包。

4 lift 指的是把物体从低处向高处"举起，抬起"。

· Could you help me **lift** this box?

你能帮我抬起这个箱子吗？

5 send 指"送，寄"。

· I can **send** this document to you.

我可以把这份文件发给你。

speak, say, tell, talk

1 speak 用作不及物动词，表示"讲话，演讲"；用作及物动词时，后接语言等。

· He can **speak** English fluently.

他英语说得很流利。

2 say 是及物动词，表示"说"，其后一般接说话的内容。

· Tom **said** that he wanted to be a doctor.

汤姆说他想成为一名医生。

3 tell 常用作及物动词，表示"告诉"，其后可以接单宾语、双宾语或复合宾语。

· He **told** me there would be a fantastic welcome party.

他告诉我会有一个非常棒的欢迎会。

4 talk 是不及物动词，表示"谈论"，侧重闲谈。

· Don't **talk** about other people.

不要随便讨论别人。

look, see, watch

1 look 侧重指看的过程，不涉及看的结果。

· She likes to **look** out of the window.

她喜欢看着窗外。

2 see 侧重看的结果，还可以引申为"明白"。

· I haven't **seen** the present you bought me.

我还没看到你给我买的礼物。

3 watch 侧重"注视，监视"，一般指的是看电视、看比赛等。

· My mother likes **watching** soap operas.

我妈妈喜欢看肥皂剧。

listen, hear

listen 是不及物动词，而且侧重听的过程，常和介词 **to** 连用。hear 是及物动词，侧重听的结果。

· I often **listen** to music for relaxation.

我经常听音乐放松。

· I **hear** someone calling for help.

我听见有人在求救。

learn, study

learn 表示"学会"，侧重指学习的结果。study 侧重指学习的过程，但是两者在表示"学"时可以互换。

· Many people know the necessity of **learning**/**studying** English.

许多人都知道学习英语的必要性。

· It took me a long time to **learn** how to use a computer.

我花了很长时间才学会如何使用电脑。

第六单元 系动词

系动词后一定要接表语，来共同构成系表结构。这种系表结构主要用来说明主语的状况、性质、特征等。

1 状态系动词主要是 **be** 动词，用来表示主语的状态、特征等。

> be 动词 are 表示 children 的状态，很开心

- The children **are** happy on the weekend.

  孩子们在周末很开心。

> be 动词 is 表示 coat 的特征，是黑色的

- This coat **is** black.

  这件外套是黑色的。

2 持续性系动词主要有 **remain**，**keep**，**stay** 等，主要用来表示主语持续的态度或状态等。

> 系动词 remain 表示 everyone 的态度，保持沉默

- Everyone **remained** silent after the teacher asked the question.

  老师问完问题后，大家都保持了沉默。

> 系动词 stay 表示 supermarket 的状态，一直开着门

- The supermarket **stays** open 24 hours a day.

  这家超市一天 24 小时营业。

3 表象性系动词主要有 **look**，**appear**，**seem** 等，表示"看起来……，似乎……"。

> 系动词 look 表示"看起来"

- She **looked** shocked when hearing the news.

  听到这个消息时，她看起来很震惊。

> 系动词 seem 表示"似乎"

- You **seem** so different from you used to.

  你看起来和以前大不一样了。

4 感官系动词主要有 **taste**，**smell**，**sound**，**feel** 等，表示人的五官感受。要注意的是，感官系动词后面接的是形容词而不是副词。

> smell 后接形容词 delicious

- The dishes **smell** delicious.

  这些菜闻起来很香。

> feel 后接形容词 cold

- It's snowing and I **feel** so cold.

  下雪了，我觉得好冷。

5 变化系动词主要有 **become**，**grow**，**turn**，**get**，**fall** 等，用来表示主语的变化。

> turn 用来表示 leaves 的变化，变绿了

- Spring is coming, and the leaves **turn** green.

  春天来了，叶子变绿了。

> become 用来表示 he 的变化，变得不健康

- Eating too much junk food, he **becomes** unhealthy.

  吃了太多的垃圾食品，他变得不健康。

become 是一个比较正式的动词，而且常用现在时和过去时表示发生的变化。
grow 表示变化，侧重指渐变的过程。
turn 侧重指变化的结果，且多指颜色的变化。

一、圈出下列句子中的系动词。

1. Some courses are compulsory, and others are optional. 有些课程是必修课，有些是选修课。

2. It is a fine day. How about we go out and play? 天气不错，我们出去玩怎么样？

3. I often work out to keep fit. 我经常锻炼身体以保持健康。

4. You appear so sad. What happened? 你看起来很伤心，发生什么事了？

5. She seems so nervous before exams. 考试前她似乎很紧张。

6. It smells weird in the fridge. 冰箱里有股怪味。

7. The sunshine makes me feel warm. 阳光使我感到温暖。

8. I was so tired and fell asleep quickly. 我太累了，很快就睡着了。

9. The cake smells sweet. 这蛋糕闻起来很甜。

10. Tomatoes grow well in the sun. 西红柿在阳光下长得很好。

二、将下列单词按照正确的顺序排序。

1. red   the   leaves   turn   maple

_____

2. so   music   the   scary   sounds

_____

3. cooking   too   your   tastes   salty

_____

4. for   the   drugstore   closed   stays   a   week

_____

5. seem   so   you   happy

_____

参考答案：

一、1. are; are   2. is   3. keep   4. appear   5. seems
　　6. smells   7. feel   8. was; fall   9. smells   10. grow

二、1. The maple leaves turn red.   2. The music sounds so scary.
　　3. Your cooking tastes too salty.   4. The drugstore stays closed for a week.
　　5. You seem so happy.

第七单元 助动词（be/do/have）

- 助动词本身不能构成单独的谓语
- 助动词可与实义动词构成其他句型
- 一个主动词不能由两个助动词来协助

be 动词

be 动词主要有 is，am，are，were，was，been，being，这些词作助动词时主要用来构成进行时态或被动语态。

现在进行时

· Your mother and your sister **are cooking** in the kitchen.
你妈妈和你姐姐正在厨房里做饭。

过去进行时

· I **was taking** a bath when you came.
你来的时候我正在洗澡。

被动语态

· The garbage **was taken out** by my sister.
垃圾是被我姐姐扔的。

do, does, did

1 助动词 do，did，does 后的主动词要用原形。

· **Do** you often **play** games after work?
你下班后经常玩游戏吗？

· **Did** you **watch** the movie *Avatar*?
你看过电影《阿凡达》吗？

· She **doesn't finish** her homework on time.
她没有按时完成家庭作业。

2 由 don't 构成的否定祈使句，不能使用 didn't 和 doesn't。

don't 构成的否定祈使句

· **Don't** speak loudly.
不要大声喧哗。

（×）Doesn't throw waste anywhere.

（√）Don't throw waste anywhere.
不要随地扔垃圾。

3 do, did, does 用来避免重复。

· — Do you know that we are going on vacation?
你知道我们要去度假吗？

do 指的是：我知道我们要去度假，用来避免重复

— Yes, I **do**.
是的，我知道。

have, has, had

作助动词时，have，has，had 是现在完成时和过去完成时的标志，没有实际意义。

现在完成时

· Mr. Smith **has finished** writing the report.
史密斯先生已经写完了报告。

过去完成时

· When we got to the station, the train **had left**.
当我们到达车站时，火车已经开走了。

表示"去过某地"用 have/has been to，而表示"去了某个地方"用 have/has gone to。

Exercise

一、请从下面方框中选择合适的助动词补全对话。

| shall |
| likely |
| are |
| would |
| did |

1. A: Have you found a solution to the project yet?

   B: Not yet. We _____ trying to look for the best solution.

2. A: What's wrong with you?

   B: I am _____ to have a fever.

3. A: Did you finish your homework?

   B: Yes, I _____.

4. A: What _____ we eat for dinner?

   B: How about noodles?

5. A: _____ you like a glass of water?

   B: Yes, please.

二、根据要求改写句子。

1. I accidentally broke the glass. （改为被动语态）

   _____

2. He was praised for doing well in the exam. （改为第一人称）

   _____

3. The man wants to leave home. （改为否定句）

   _____

4. The project has been finished. （改为否定句）

   _____

5. People grow corn in the north of the states. （改为被动语态）

   _____

参考答案：

一、1. are   2. likely   3. did   4. shall   5. Would

二、1. The glass was broken by me accidentally.

   2. I was praised for doing well in the exam.

   3. The man doesn't want to leave home.

   4. The project hasn't been finished yet.

   5. Corn is grown in the north of the states by people.

第八单元　情态动词（can/may/must/need/should）

can

can 用于表示客观能力和可能性。它用来询问是否可以做某事或请求做某事，其过去式是 could。在口语中，用 could 进行询问是为了表达委婉的语气。can 的否定形式 can't 常用来表示某种情况是不可能的。

can 表示能力

• He **can** run quickly in the sprint race.
他可以在短跑比赛中跑得很快。

can 表示请求

• **Can** you do me a favor and close the door?
你能帮我一个忙，把门关上吗？

could 表示委婉的语气

• **Could** you please turn it down?
你能把声音关小点吗？

can't 表示这件事是不可能的

• This bag **can't** belong to Tom, for his is white.
这个包不可能是汤姆的，因为他的是白色的。

may

may 可以表示请求、允许、推测。may 引导的疑问句，其肯定回答用 may，否定回答用 can't。may 的过去式是 might，它比 may 的语气更委婉。

may 表示请求

• **May** you lend me some money?
你可以借给我一些钱吗？

may 表示推测

• My computer **may** have been stolen.
我的电脑可能被偷了。

must

must 表示肯定的推测、必须、必要。它侧重于因义务、责任、命令等必须要做某事，更偏向客观性。must 引导的疑问句，其肯定回答用 must，否定回答用 needn't 或 don't/doesn't have to。must 的否定形式 mustn't 表示"不允许、禁止"。

must 表示肯定的推测

• It **must** be my little brother crying.
一定是我弟弟在哭。

must 表示必须

• You **must** wash your hands before eating.
你吃饭前必须洗手。

mustn't 表示不允许、禁止

• You **mustn't** make noise in public.
你不能在公共场合吵闹。

• — **Must** I go back to school before three o'clock?
我必须在三点前回学校吗？
— Yes, you **must**.
是的，必须。
— No, you **needn't**/**don't have to**.
不，你不必。

need

need 表示"需要"，常用在疑问句和否定句中。 **need** 的否定形式是 **needn't** 表示"不需要"。

need 用于疑问句中
- **Need** I bring some snacks?
  我需要带些零食吗？

need 用于否定句中
- I **needn't** go to the station in a hurry.
  我不需要急急忙忙去车站。

should

should 表示按照常理的"应该"，也可以表示建议。**should** 有时还可以表示惊奇，意为"竟然"。

should 表示应该
- It **should** be rainy tomorrow.
  明天应该会下雨。

should 表示建议
- You **should** change your mind.
  你应该改变主意。

should 表示惊奇
- You **should** fail to pass the interview.
  你竟然没有通过面试。

Exercise

一、根据括号内的情态动词改写句子。

1. The train is late. (might) The train might be late.

2. My father quits smoking. (must) _____

3. You left your keys on the table. (may) _____

4. Tom is good at swimming. (can) _____

5. You fill out the documents in a week. (should) _____

二、为下列句子勾选正确的情态动词。

1. You ○ **should** ○ **can** be careful during the exam.

2. ○ **Must** ○ **Can** I join the art club?

3. ○ **Could** ○ **Must** I borrow your computer?

4. It's not a big deal. You ○ **need** ○ **needn't** worry.

5. Some small companies ○ **may** ○ **must** close because of the economic crisis.

参考答案：
一、2. My father must quit smoking.   3. You may have left your keys on the table.
   4. Tom can swim very well.   5. You should fill out the documents in a week.
二、1. should   2. Can   3. Could   4. needn't   5. may

第九单元 非谓语动词 1：动词不定式

1 动词不定式在句中可以作主语、宾语、表语、定语、状语和独立成分。在作主语的时候，可以用形式主语 it 来代替，且谓语动词用单数形式。

真正的主语

- It's very important **to be friendly to others**.
  与人友善是很重要的。

作宾语

- I'm ready **to spend** my holiday.
  我准备好去度假了。

作表语

- My aim is **to win** the first prize.
  我的目标是赢得第一名。

作定语

- I have a lot of work **to do**.
  我有很多工作要做。

作结果状语

- They got to the station only **to find** the train had left.
  他们赶到车站，却发现火车已经离开了。

2 大多数动词后如果再接另一个动词，要接动词的不定式。

afford	agree	appear
arrange	ask	care
decide	expect	fail
hope	manage	mean
offer	plan	prepare
pretend	promise	refuse
seem	want	

3 不带 to 的不定式

⊙ 在两个并列的不定式短语中，第二个不定式可以省略 to。

go 前面省略了 to

- I want to go swimming and **go** fishing.
  我想去游泳和钓鱼。

⊙ 表示建议或命令的口语中，go 和 come 后可以接不带 to 的不定式。

drink 前面省略了 to

- Go/Come **drink** a glass of water.
  去 / 来喝杯水吧。

⊙ 接不带 to 的不定式短语

cannot but	cannot choose but
cannot help but	would rather
other than	had better

We have nothing to **do** but **sleep**.
除了睡觉，我们无事可做。

We have no choice but **to** sleep.
除了睡觉，我们别无选择。

连词 but 之前如果有实义动词 do，那么 but 后面的不定式不要 to。但是如果 but 前没有实义动词 do，那么 but 后面的不定式前要加 to。

4 有些动词后既可以接动名词也可以接不定式，意义区别不大。

begin	continue
like	love
prefer	start

- I <u>began to play</u> the violin when I was ten years old.

  = began playing

  我十岁的时候就开始拉小提琴了。

- I <u>love to</u> eat junk food.

  = love eating

  我很爱吃垃圾食品。

Exercise

一、从下面四个选项中选出最佳答案。

1. She opened the window _____ what the weather was like.

    A. see   B. to see   C. seeing   D. saw

2. It's a good idea _____ things in advance.

    A. prepare   B. to prepare   C. preparing   D. prepared

3. I cannot choose but _____ you the truth.

    A. tell   B. to tell   C. telling   D. told

4. I have nothing to do but _____ pictures.

    A. take   B. to take   C. taking   D. took

5. I don't want to play games or _____ out.

    A. go   B. to go   C. going   D. gone

二、用括号中所给词的正确形式填空。

1. We promise _____ (deliver) it within 24 hours.

2. I have no choice but _____ (beg) you.

3. My little son would rather _____ (play) than study.

4. I can't afford _____ (buy) this car.

5. She couldn't refuse_____ (help) this poor man.

参考答案：

一、1. B   2. B   3. B   4. A   5. A

二、1. to deliver   2. to beg   3. play   4. to buy   5. to help

第十单元　非谓语动词 2：动名词

1 用作主语，表示抽象或者习惯性动作。

Swimming is my favorite sport. 游泳是我最喜欢的运动。

Learning is important for students. 学习对学生来说很重要。

> 不定式作主语，表示具体的、一次性的动作。

2 动名词作主语可以用 it 作形式主语，把动名词放在句末，主要用于一些固定句型中。

It's no good/use doing ... 做……没有用

It's a shame doing ... 做……是可耻的

It's fun doing ... 做……很有趣

It's a waste of time doing ... 做……浪费时间

3 动名词作宾语

及物动词

admit	advise	avoid	celebrate
consider	delay	deny	dislike
enjoy	envy	escape	fancy
finish	imagine	involve	mind
miss	pardon	postpone	practice
resist	risk	stand	suffer

• I enjoy walking in the rain.

　我喜欢在雨中漫步。

动词短语

be afraid of	be tired of	can't help
feel like	give up	insist on
keep on	lead to	think of
look forward to	put off	

• When the clown performs, the children can't help laughing.

　小丑表演的时候，孩子们开怀大笑。

有些动词后既可以接动名词也可以接不定式，有的意义差别很大。

remember doing sth 记得做过某事
remember to do sth 记得要去做某事

forget doing sth 忘记做过某事
forget to do sth 忘记要去做某事

mean doing sth 意味着做某事
mean to do sth 打算做某事

try doing sth 尝试做某事
try to do sth 尽力做某事

stop doing sth 停止一直做的事情
stop to do sth 停下来去做其他某事

4 动名词一般有一般式和完成式，而且均有被动语态。在动名词的一般式中，其表示的动作和谓语动词的动作既可同时发生，也可发生在谓语动词的动作之前或之后。在动名词的完成式中，其表示的动作发生在谓语动词的动作之前。

一般式，saw 和 being stolen 同时发生

• I saw that girl's wallet **being stolen**.

我看到那个女孩的钱包被偷了。

完成式，having finished 发生在 remember 之前

• I remember **having finished** the report.

我记得已经完成了报告。

Exercise

为下列句子勾选正确的答案。

1. Don't forget ○ **to do** ○ **doing** your homework in the evening.

2. It's no good ○ **to complain** ○ **complaining** now.

3. Let's stop ○ **to have** ○ **having** a rest.

4. We are afraid of ○ **to try** ○ **trying** something new.

5. They insist on ○ **to play** ○ **playing** games at night.

6. I'm looking forward ○ **to receive** ○ **to receiving** your answer.

7. He admitted ○ **to have** ○ **having** copied other people's answers.

8. It's no use ○ **to call** ○ **calling** him now.

9. I try my best ○ **to meet** ○ **meeting** your requirement.

10. She denied ○ **to take** ○ **taking** away my wallet.

参考答案：

1. to do   2. complaining   3. to have   4. trying   5. playing
6. to receiving   7. having   8. calling   9. to meet   10. taking

第十一单元 非谓语动词 3：现在分词

1 现在分词作定语。

singing 用来修饰 girl

- The girl **singing** on the stage is my best friend.

  在舞台上唱歌的那个女孩是我最好的朋友。

有些动词的现在分词形式只用作形容词，如：interesting 有趣的，exciting 令人兴奋的，surprising 令人惊讶的，amazing 令人惊异的，boring 无聊的等。

2 现在分词作表语。

boiling 作表语

- The water is **boiling** and would you pour me a glass of water?

  水开了，给我倒杯水好吗？

3 现在分词作状语表示时间、条件、原因、结果、让步、方式等。

作状语，表示时间

- **Having left my hometown**, I missed my parents very much.

  离开了家乡，我非常想念我的父母。

作状语，表示地点。

- **Seeing from the top of the mountain**, you will see beautiful scenery.

  从山顶上看，你会看到美丽的景色。

作状语，表示结果

- I fell, **hitting my head** against the door.

  我摔倒了，头撞在了门上。

作状语，表示方式

- My flight delayed, so I killed time **sleeping**.

  我的航班晚点了，所以我睡觉打发时间。

4 现在分词作宾语补足语。

作宾语补足语

- I saw him **working** in the garden.

  我看见他在花园里干活。

有些动词后可以接现在分词作宾语补足语。如：see 看见，watch 看，hear 听见，feel 觉得，find 发现，get 让，使，keep 保持，notice 注意，observe 观察，listen to 听。

一、找出下列句子的错误之处并改正。

1. I find it amazed that you didn't pass the exam. _____

2. I hear the birds sang in the trees now. _____

3. Seeing from the airline, humans look like ants. _____

4. Be ill, she didn't go to work yesterday. _____

5. My father died, left nothing but debt. _____

6. Study hard, you will get good grades. _____

7. Have failed many times, she lost her heart. _____

8. Who is the boy to play basketball? _____

9. On heard the news, all the children jumped with joy. _____

10. He entered the hall, held a camera. _____

二、圈出下列句子中的现在分词，并判断在句中作什么成分。

1. The children talking to strangers study in Class Four.

2. The story is so interesting.

3. We all found the film boring.

4. When waiting for the train, I got nothing to do.

5. Eating so much, Tom feels uncomfortable.

参考答案:

一、1. amazed → amazing   2. sang → singing   3. Seeing → Seen

4. Be → Being   5. left → leaving   6. Study → Studying   7. Have → Having

8. to play → playing   9. heard → hearing   10. held → holding

二、1. talking 作定语   2. interesting 作表语   3. boring 作宾语补足语

4. waiting 作时间状语   5. Eating 作原因状语

第十二单元 非谓语动词 4：现在分词和动名词的区别

现在分词作定语强调的是状态，而动名词作定语强调的是目的或用途。

a sleeping boy 一个睡着的男孩

（现在分词强调的是人的状态）

the swimming pool 游泳池

（动名词强调的是池子的用途）

wearing 是现在分词

- The man **wearing** leather jacket is my little brother.

  穿皮夹克的那个人是我弟弟。

  being in red 是动名词短语

- **Being in red** at the funeral is improper.

  在葬礼上穿红色衣服是不合适的。

现在分词作表语强调特点，而动名词作表语强调的是一件事。

amazing 是现在分词，表示特点

- The gift you give me is **amazing**.

  你给我的礼物太棒了。

  playing 是动名词，表示一件事

- What I want to do is **playing** games.

  我想做的事是玩游戏。

现在分词不能作主语和宾语，而动名词可以。

telling 是动名词，作 mind 的宾语

- I don't mind **telling** you the truth.

  我不介意告诉你真相。

playing 是动名词，作主语

- **Playing** by the seaside is very fun.

  在海边玩很有趣。

 **Exercise**

将下列短语按要求进行分类。

a sleeping girl

a sleeping bag

a swimming suit

a swimming boy

a flying bird

the smiling face

the reading material

a hiding place

a writing desk

a barking dog

现在分词

动名词

参考答案:

现在分词: a sleeping girl

a swimming boy

a flying bird

the smiling face

a barking dog

动名词: a sleeping bag

a swimming suit

the reading material

a hiding place

a writing desk

第十三单元 非谓语动词 5：过去分词

过去分词既有动词的性质，也有形容词的性质。它表示已经发生的动作，而且有被动意味。

1 过去分词作定语，单词过去分词一般放在被修饰词之前，过去分词短语一般放在被修饰词之后。

tired 作定语，放在被修饰词 worker 的前面

- The **tired** worker was motionless.
这个疲倦的工人一动不动。

known for tea 作定语，放在被修饰词 city 的后面

- The city **known for tea** attracts many people.
这座以茶叶闻名的城市吸引了很多人。

2 过去分词作表语与被动语态的区别：作表语的过去分词具有形容词的性质，一般表示状态，而被动语态一般表示动作。

written 是表语，表示状态

- His new novel is well **written**.
他的新小说写得很好。

written 是被动语态，表示动作

- The new novel was **written** by him.
这部新小说是他写的。

3 过去分词作宾语补足语。

relaxed 作宾语 yourself 的补足语

- Try to make yourself **relaxed**.
试着让你自己放松。

过去分词有时还可作 with 短语中的宾语补足语。
With the computer bought, she began to play games.
买了电脑，她就开始玩游戏了。

4 过去分词作状语表示让步、条件、原因、方式等。

frightened 表示让步

- **Frightened** by a dog, he still dared to approach one.
虽然他被狗吓坏了，但还敢靠近狗。

given 表示条件

- **Given** more money, I would be happier.
如果给我更多钱，我会更开心。

Exercise

结合图片，用括号中所给词的正确形式填空。

1. When I got there, the store _____ (close) by the clerk.

2. _____ (lose) in thought, he didn't hear your voice.

3. The woman came in, _____ (follow) by some reporters.

4. _____ (give) more time, I would have finished the test very well.

5. He felt _____ (satisfy) with his performance.

6. With everything _____ (arrange), he went to work.

7. I read a lot of novels _____ (write) by Lu Xun.

8. With the shoes _____ (wear) out, she has to throw them away.

9. A man, _____ (dress) like a gentleman, came in the office.

10. _____ (move) by the new movie, I can't help crying.

参考答案：

1. was closed   2. Lost   3. followed   4. Given   5. satisfied
6. arranged   7. written   8. worn   9. dressed   10. Moved

第九章

基本句式
Basic Sentences

第一单元 陈述句

陈述句 { 肯定陈述句，即肯定句
         否定陈述句，即否定句

- I am leaving for the airport at 5:00 tomorrow afternoon. (肯定句)
  我明天下午五点去机场。
- I don't want to work overtime. (否定句)
  我不想加班。

肯定句

1 肯定句用来说明、提出某件事或看法等。

- Red looks more energetic and good-looking than black.
  红色比黑色看起来更有活力、更好看。
- Everyone was against the plan she put forward. 每个人都反对她提出的计划。

2 宾语从句要用陈述语序。

- My wife asked me **when I could go home at night**.
  我妻子问我晚上什么时候可以回家。
- Did you know **she was late for school yesterday**?
  你知道她昨天上学迟到了吗？

否定句

形式：

{ be 动词 + not
  助动词 / 情态动词 + not
  do/does/did + not + 实义动词原形

- I'm not their elected supervisor.
  我不是他们选出来的主管。
- She shouldn't go to school by car.
  她不应该坐车去学校。
- I don't often play games at night.
  我晚上不经常玩游戏。

否定句的用法

1 句中有 **neither，nor，little，few，too ... to ...，hardly** 等词时即为否定句。

- There is **little** food in the fridge.
  冰箱里几乎没有食物了。
- The shoes are **too** small for me **to** wear.
  这双鞋太小了，我穿不了。

如果否定句中有 some, both, always, all 等词，则构成部分否定，意为"不一定都……"或"不完全……"等。全部否定要用 neither, nobody, none, nothing 等词。
All the students **don't** perform well in study.
并不是所有学生都能学习好。
No one will look down on you.
没有人会看不起你。

2 一般来说，一个否定句中只有一个否定词。

- He did **not** go to school yesterday because he was ill.

  他昨天因为生病没去上学。

3 两个否定词一起使用就构成了"双重否定表肯定"。

> 即：所有人都愿意参加会议

- **No one** is **unwilling** to attend the meeting.

  没有人不愿意参加会议。

> 即：这种事很常见

- It is **not uncommon** for this matter to happen.

  这种事的发生并不少见。

4 还有一种情况是含蓄否定，也称意义否定。这种否定指的是用某些肯定词汇表示否定含义，这样的词有 **fail, neglect, absence, the last, ignore, too ... to ...** 等。

- She **failed** the English exam again.

  她英语考试又没及格。

- **The last** person I want to see is Caroline.

  我最不想见到的人就是卡洛琳。

肯定句变否定句的特殊情况

1 句中的 **and** 要变为 **or**。

- I like playing the guitar **and** piano.

  我喜欢弹吉他和钢琴。

- I don't like playing the guitar **or** piano.

  我不喜欢弹吉他和钢琴。

2 句中的 **some**（或 **some** 和其他词组成的复合词）要变为 **any**（或 **any** 和其他词组成的复合词）。

- My father bought **some** strawberries.

  我爸爸买了一些草莓。

- My father didn't buy **any** strawberries.

  我爸爸没有买（任何）草莓。

3 句中的 **already** 要变为 **yet**，且 **already** 多位于助动词之后，**yet** 多位于句尾。

- I have **already** finished my homework.

  我已经完成了作业。

- I haven't finished my homework **yet**.

  我还没有完成作业。

第二单元 感叹句

what 引导的感叹句

What + a/an +（形容词）+ 可数名词的单数形式 +（主语 + 谓语）!
What +（形容词）+ 可数名词的复数形式 / 不可数名词 +（主语 + 谓语）!

• **What** a beautiful <u>day</u> (it is)!
多么美好的一天!

• **What** noisy <u>children</u> (they are)!
多么吵闹的孩子啊!

• **What** delicious <u>orange juice</u> (it is)!
多么美味的橙汁啊!

how 引导的感叹句

How +（形容词）+ a/an + 可数名词的单数形式 +（主语 + 谓语）!
How + 形容词 / 副词 +（主语 + 谓语）!
How + 主语 + 谓语!

• **How** beautiful a wall lamp (it is)!
多么漂亮的壁灯啊!

• **How** slow (you run)!
你跑得多么慢啊!

• **How** time flies!
时间过得真快!

> what 引导的感叹句和 how 引导的感叹句可互换。
> What a lovely girl she is! = How lovely a girl she is!
> 她是一个多么可爱的女孩啊!

其他形式的感叹句

1 **that** 引导的感叹句，此类感叹句多表示愿望、遗憾。

• **That** I could see you again!
我多么想能再看到你!

2 短语感叹句。

• **My god!** 我的天啊!

3 **may** 开头的感叹句，此类感叹句多表示愿望。

• **May** you succeed at music!
祝你在音乐方面取得成功!

4 **who** 引导的感叹句，此类感叹句多表示惊奇。

• **Who** would have ever thought it!
谁会想到呢!

5 即使是否定疑问句也表示肯定意义。

• **Didn't he** run away from home!
他离家出走了!

6 句中有 **so** 和 **such** 时也可作感叹句。

• You are **so** stupid!
你真笨啊!

7 **if/if only** 引导的感叹句。

• **If only** you were here!
你要是在这儿就好了!

Exercise

将下面陈述句转换成 **what** 和 **how** 引导的感叹句。

1. The weather is hot.

_____   _____

2. These flowers are flourishing.

_____   _____

3. Tom is a handsome boy.

_____   _____

4. He is a great pianist.

_____   _____

5. It's a heavy rain.

_____   _____

6. The breakfast is so hearty.

_____   _____

7. It's a boring film.

_____   _____

8. The idea is useful.

_____   _____

参考答案：

1. What hot weather it is!   How hot the weather is!
2. What flourishing flowers they are!   How flourishing these flowers are!
3. What a handsome boy Tom is!   How handsome a boy Tom is!
4. What a great pianist he is!   How great a pianist he is!
5. What a heavy rain it is!   How heavy the rain is!
6. What a hearty breakfast it is!   How hearty the breakfast is!
7. What a boring film it is!   How boring a film it is!
8. What a useful idea it is!   How useful an idea it is!

第三单元 祈使句

祈使句也称命令句，是用来表示命令、请求、警告、劝告、禁止等的句子。与普通句子不同的是，祈使句通常以动词原形开头。

分类

1 第二人称祈使句，它的祈使对象是 **you**，但在句中常省略。第二人称祈使句也可以加上主语或加 **do**，此时表示强调。

- **Be** quiet! 保持安静！
  = **You** be quiet! 你安静点。
- **Do** remember to turn off the light.
  一定要记得关灯。

2 第一、三人称祈使句，以 **let** 开头，后面的动词用原形，祈使对象用宾格形式。要表示强调，也可在句首加 **do**。

第一人称祈使句
- **Let me** play computer games for a while.
  让我玩一会儿电脑游戏吧。

第三人称祈使句
- **Let them** pack their own bags.
  让他们自己收拾行李。

表示强调
- **Do** let Nancy call me back.
  一定要让南希给我回电话。

3 其他形式的祈使句
- No parking. 禁止停车。
- No smoking. 禁止抽烟。
- Faster. 快点。

使祈使句语气更加委婉的方法

1 在表示请求时可在句首或句末加上 **please**。

- **Please** turn the volume down.
  请把声音调低点。
- Lend me your computer, **please**.
  请借我用一下你的电脑。

2 在句末加上问句 **will you**，这样语气会更加委婉。

- Be careful, **will you**?
  小心点，好吗？

祈使句的否定形式

第一、三人称的否定句的形式是 **Don't let ...** 或 **Let ... not ...**；第二人称祈使句的否定形式是在句首加上否定词 **don't**，**never** 等。

第一人称祈使句的否定形式
- **Let's not** make a decision in a hurry.
  我们不要匆忙做决定。

第三人称祈使句的否定形式
- **Don't let** her know the truth.
  别让她知道真相。

第二人称祈使句的否定形式
- **Don't** eat too much. 不要吃太多。

第二人称祈使句的否定形式
- **Never** talk like that again.
  别再那样说话了。

将下列句子转换为祈使句。

1. You shouldn't stay up late playing games.

_____

2. I invite you to the welcome party.

_____

3. You should be there on time.

_____

4. You should clean the classroom.

_____

5. You mustn't drive so fast.

_____

6. We mustn't smoke in public.

_____

7. You should keep quiet in the library.

_____

8. We mustn't climb the rocks in the park.

_____

参考答案：

1. Don't stay up late playing games.
2. Come to the welcome party (, please/will you?).
3. Please be there on time.
4. Clean the classroom.
5. Don't drive so fast.
6. Don't smoke in public.
7. Keep quiet in the library.
8. Don't climb the rocks in the park.

第四单元 一般疑问句和选择疑问句

句中含有 be 动词 / 情态动词的一般疑问句

结构: "be 动词 + 主语 + 其他成分?"或"情态动词 + 主语 + 动词原形 + 其他成分?"。

回答: Yes, 主语 +be 动词 / 情态动词;No, 主语 +be 动词 / 情态动词 +not;表肯定或否定意义的副词(词组)。

否定形式: be 动词 / 情态动词 + not + 主语 + 其他成分?。

- — **Are** you a math teacher?

  你是一名数学老师吗?

  — Yes, I am.

  是的,我是。(肯定回答)

  — No, I'm not.

  不,我不是。(否定回答)

  — Certainly.

  当然了。

- **Aren't** you a teacher? 你不是一名老师吗?

- **Can't** you get there on time? 你不能准时到那里吗?

- — **Can** you play the guitar?

  你会弹吉他吗?

  — Yes, I can.

  是的,我会。(肯定回答)

  — No, I can't.

  不,我不会。(否定回答)

  — Certainly.

  当然了。

> 用表示肯定含义的副词回答,此时后面可以不加其他成分。

句中含有实义动词的一般疑问句

结构: "助动词 + 主语 + 动词原形 + 其他成分?"。

回答: Yes, 主语 +be 动词 / 情态动词;No, 主语 +be 动词 / 情态动词 +not;表肯定或否定意义的副词(词组)。

否定形式: "助动词 + not + 主语 + 动词原形 + 其他成分?"。

- — **Do** you know the song? 你知道这首歌吗?

  — Yes, I do. 是的,我知道。(肯定回答)

  — No, I don't. 不,我不知道。(否定回答)

  — Certainly. 当然了。

- **Doesn't** she always hang out with you?

  她不是经常和你一块出去玩吗?

> 在一般疑问句中,如果要表达"一些",则用 any。但是,如果一般疑问句中要用"一些"来修饰表示"建议、请求"等交际功能的词语时,就要用 some。
>
> Do you have **any** opinions on this matter? 你对这件事有什么看法吗?
>
> 表示"建议、请求",用 some
>
> Can you give me **some** useful advice? 你可以给我一些有用的建议吗?

选择疑问句

1 句中有两种或两种以上的条件可供对方选择，中间用 **or** 连接。

· Do you like playing soccer **or** basketball?

你喜欢踢足球还是打篮球？

2 选择疑问句中的选择部分也可以用 **or not** 表示。

· Is the glass of water cool **or not**?

这杯水凉不凉？

· Do you like the story **or not**?

你喜不喜欢这个故事？

· Is the weather hot **or not**?

这天气热不热？

3 如果 **or** 后面的选择部分有不定冠词 **a/an**，则不能省略。

· Is Tina a teacher **or a** lawyer?

蒂娜是一名老师还是律师？

4 对选择疑问句进行回答时不能用 **yes/no**，而是必须从所提供的选项中进行选择，也可以否定或肯定所有选项。

· — Do you like bananas, apples or oranges?

你喜欢香蕉、苹果还是橘子？

— I like bananas and oranges.

我喜欢香蕉和橘子。（选择某些选项）

— I like all of them.

我都喜欢。（肯定所有选项）

— None. 我都不喜欢。（否定所有选项）

Exercise

根据提示，回答下面的一般疑问句，完成句子。

1. — Are you reading now?

— Yes, _____.

2. — Can you sing?

— No, _____.

3. — Did you go to the library?

— No, _____.

4. — Is Tina going shopping?

— Yes, _____.

参考答案：

1. I am　2. I can't　3. I didn't　4. she is

第五单元 特殊疑问句

1 特殊疑问句以特殊疑问词开头，结构一般是"特殊疑问词 + 一般疑问句？"。

when 什么时候	where 哪里
why 为什么	what 什么
who 谁	whose 谁的
which 哪个	how 怎么

- **Where** did you meet?
  你们在哪里遇到的？

- **How often** do you exercise?
  你多久锻炼一次？

"why + 一般疑问句的否定形式"结构有时可以表示劝告、建议等。其结构为"why not + 动词原形 + 其他成分"或"why don't you + 动词原形 + 其他成分"。

Why not put down the phone?
= **Why don't you** put down the phone?
你为什么不放下手机呢？

2 与一般疑问句不同，对特殊疑问句进行回答时不能用 yes/no，而要问什么答什么。

- — **Where** did you find my key?
  你在哪里找到我的钥匙的？
- — I found it on the tea table.
  我在茶几上找到的。

3 特殊疑问句可以有一个以上的特殊疑问词。

When and where shall we meet?
我们什么时候在哪里见面？

4 一些常用特殊疑问词的用法。

◎ **when** 是对时间的提问，表示"什么时候"。

- **When** was the building built?
  这座建筑是什么时候建成的？

◎ **where** 是对地点的提问，表示"在哪里"。

- **Where** are you from?
  你从哪里来的？

◎ **why** 是对原因的提问，表示"为什么"。

- **Why** are you late?
  你为什么迟到了？

◎ **who** 是对人的提问，表示"谁"。

- **Who** gave you this gift?
  谁给你的礼物？

◎ **whose** 是对物体所属的提问，表示"谁的"。

- **Whose** cup did you break?
  你打碎的是谁的杯子？

◎ **which** 是对目标的提问，表示"哪个 / 哪些"。

- **Which** bag is yours?
  哪个包是你的？

◎ what 是对动词和名词的提问,表示"什么"。

• **What** color do you like best?
你最喜欢什么颜色?

◎ **how** 是对方式和程度的提问,表示"怎么,怎样"。

• **How** do you go to school?
你怎样去学校?

◎ **how many** 对可数名词的数量进行提问,**how much** 对不可数名词的数量提问。

• **How many** tickets do you have?
你有多少张票?

• **How much** housework do you have?
你有多少家务活?

how much 还能对价格进行提问,表示"多少钱"。

◎ **how long** 是对长度的提问,表示"多长",它既能表示"物体的长度",也能表示"时间的长度"。

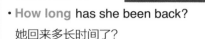

• **How long** is the bridge?
这座桥有多长?

• **How long** has she been back?
她回来多长时间了?

◎ **how often** 是对频率的提问,表示"多长时间一次"。

• **How often** do you go to the supermarket?
你多久去一次超市?

◎ **how soon** 是对将来时间的提问,表示"多快,多久"。

• **How soon** will you be back?
你多久能回来?

Exercise

选择合适的特殊疑问词填空,补全句子。

1. _____ is your favorite actor?

2. _____ don't you ask my advice?

3. _____ club do you want to join?

4. _____ do you go to the cinema?

5. _____ will it cost?

6. _____ will the flight take?

参考答案:
1. Who   2. Why   3. Which   4. How often   5. How much   6. How long

第六单元 反义疑问句

基本形式

前肯后否和前否后肯

当陈述部分是肯定句时，肯定回答用"Yes + 肯定式"，意为"是的，……"；否定回答用"No + 否定式"，意为"不是，……"。

当陈述部分是否定句时，肯定回答用"Yes + 肯定式"，意为"不是，……"；否定回答用"No + 否定式"，意为"是的，……"。

- — You're **not** good at figures, **are** you?

  你不擅长算数，对吗？

  — No, I'm not. 是的，我不擅长。

  — Yes, I am. 不是，我擅长。

特定用法

1 陈述句中有否定前缀或否定后缀的词时，当肯定句处理。这样的词有 **dislike，unhealthy，careless，aimless** 等。

- He **dislikes** eating vegetables, **doesn't he**?

  他不喜欢吃蔬菜，不是吗？

2 陈述句中有表示否定意义的词时，当否定句处理。这样的词有 **no，nobody，never，rarely，not** 等。

- You have **never** seen such a wonderful film, **have you**?

  你从来没有看过这么精彩的电影，是吗？

3 陈述句的主语是 **everyone/everybody/someone/somebody/anyone/no one/nobody/those/these** 或是 **these/those** 修饰的名词时，疑问句主语用 **they**。

- **Everyone** has a chance to win, don't **they**?

  每个人都有机会赢，不是吗？

- **Those** people are noisy, aren't **they**?

  那些人很吵，不是吗？

4 陈述句部分是祈使句时，分为三种情况：

◉ 陈述部分是省去主语的祈使句时，疑问句要用 **will/won't you**。

Come and sit down, **won't you**?

来坐下，好吗？

◉ 陈述部分是 **Let's** 开头的祈使句时，疑问句要用 **shall we**。

Let's go shopping together, **shall we**?

我们一起去购物吧，好吗？

◉ 陈述部分是 **Let us** 开头的祈使句时，疑问句要用 **will you**。

Let us play computer games for a while, **will you**?

让我们玩一会儿电脑游戏，好吗？

5 陈述句的主语是 **this/that** 所修饰的名词或是 **this/that/anything/something/everything** 时，疑问句主语用 **it**。

- **Everything** goes smoothly, isn't **it**?
  一切都很顺利，不是吗？
- **This** is a wonderful novel, isn't **it**?
  这是一本精彩的小说，不是吗？

6 陈述句中的谓语动词是 **wish** 时表示征求对方的意见，此时疑问句要用 **may**。

- I **wish** you take this matter seriously, **may** I?
  我希望你能认真对待这件事，可以吗？

7 陈述句是 **There be** 句型时，后面的疑问句部分分为两种情况：

⊙ **be** 动词前面没有助动词时，疑问句用 "**be** 动词 + **not** + **there?**"。

- There **is** a dog in the yard, **isn't there**?
  院子里有一只狗，不是吗？

⊙ **be** 动词前有助动词时，疑问句用 "助动词 + **not** + **there?**"。

- There **will be** a new library, **won't there**?
  那里将会有一个新图书馆，不是吗？

 **Exercise**

从下面四个选项中选出最佳答案。

1. You don't like eating popcorn, _____?
   A. are you   B. aren't you   C. do you   D. don't you

2. Everyone enjoys the party, _____?
   A. will you   B. don't you   C. do they   D. don't they

3. Everything is kept in good order, _____?
   A. isn't it   B. aren't you   C. don't they   D.doesn't she

4. That is incorrect, _____?
   A. isn't it   B. aren't you   C. don't they   D. doesn't she

5. There is something wrong, _____?
   A. is it   B. isn't there   C. aren't you   D. don't they

参考答案：
1. C   2. D   3. A   4. A   5. B

第十章

简单句
Simple Sentences

第一单元　**主语＋谓语**

第二单元　**主语＋系动词＋表语**

第三单元　**主语＋谓语＋宾语**

第四单元　**主语＋谓语＋间接宾语＋直接宾语**

第五单元　**主语＋谓语＋宾语＋宾语补足语**

第一单元 主语 + 谓语

> "主语 + 谓语",此结构既可以是"一个主语 + 一个谓语",也可以是"若干主语 + 若干谓语"。这种句型中的动词大多数都是不及物动词,不及物动词后边不能直接加宾语。

1 主谓结构后面没有宾语。

· **My right arm hurts**.
　　主语　　　谓语

我右胳膊疼。

· **The doctors have arrived**.
　　主语　　　　　谓语

医生们已经到了。

2 主谓结构的拓展结构。

◎ 主语 + 谓语 + 副词

· **Bella laughs loudly.**
　主语　　谓语　　副词

贝拉笑得很大声。

· Did **you sleep well**?
　　　主语　谓语　副词

你睡得好吗?

> 英语中的副词包含:
> 时间副词
> today, yesterday, tomorrow
> 地点副词
> there, here, home
> 频率副词
> usually, sometimes, often
> 程度副词
> rather, quite, almost
> 方式副词
> quickly, slowly, carefully, loudly

◎ 主语 + 谓语 + 介词短语

· **My parents live in the countryside**.
　　主语　　　谓语　　　介词短语

我父母住在乡下。

· I **haven't slept for two days**.
主语　　谓语　　　介词短语

我已经两天没睡觉了。

◎ 主语 + 谓语 + 动词不定式

· **The girl is running to catch a butterfly**.
　主语　　　谓语　　　动词不定式

这个女孩正跑着去抓一只蝴蝶。

◎ Here/There + 谓语 + 主语

· Here **comes the teacher**. 老师来了。
　　　谓语　　主语

· There **goes the train**. 火车开走了。
　　　谓语　　主语

Exercise

判断下面的句子是否为主谓结构。是的在句子的后面打"√"，不是的打"×"。

1. My stomach hurts. （ ）
   我的肚子疼。
2. Mr. Green talked excitedly. （ ）
   格林特先生激动地说着。

3. I ran to catch the bus. （ ）
   我跑着去赶公交车。
4. My brother has a bad cold. （ ）
   我弟弟患了重感冒。

5. There lies a library. （ ）
   这里有一个图书馆。
6. I bought a skirt for my daughter. （ ）
   我给女儿买了一条短裙。

7. She doesn't like English. （ ）
   她不喜欢英语。
8. She made a living by begging. （ ）
   她以乞讨为生。

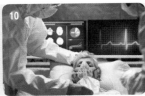

9. Max is good at playing basketball. （ ）
   马克斯擅长打篮球。
10. My grandfather is in hospital. （ ）
    我爷爷住院了。

参考答案：
1. √ 2. √ 3. √ 4. × 5. √ 6. × 7. × 8. × 9. × 10. ×

147

第二单元 主语 + 系动词 + 表语

系动词是用来辅助主语的，不能单独使用。表语主要用来修饰主语，名词、形容词、介词短语等在句中都可以充当表语。

主系表结构 ——
- I am a girl.
  我是一个女孩。
- Bella is beautiful.
  贝拉很漂亮。
- The cake tastes delicious.
  这蛋糕尝起来很美味。

主系表结构中系动词的分类

1 表示状态的系动词：be 动词。
- Your brother is handsome.
  主语　　系动词　表语
  你哥哥很帅。

2 表示持续的系动词：remain（仍然是），hold（保持），stand（保持），keep（保持）， stay（保持）等。
- You should remain calm.
  主语　　　　　系动词　表语
  你应该保持冷静。

3 表示"看起来，似乎"的系动词：look（看起来），seem（似乎），appear（似乎）等。
- You two seem happy.
  主语同位语　系动词　表语
  你们两个看起来很高兴。

4 表示感官的系动词：feel（摸起来），sound（听起来），smell（闻起来），taste（尝起来）等。
- The apple tastes sweet.
  主语　　系动词　表语
  这苹果吃起来很甜。

表示感官的动词并不全是系动词，像watch（观看），see（看见），hear（听见）等不是系动词，而是实义动词。

5 表示结果的系动词：prove（证明），turn out（结果是……）等。
- The data prove wrong.
  主语　　系动词　表语
  数据证明是错误的。

6 表示变化的系动词：become（成为），get（得到），go（变得），grow（成长），turn（变成）等。
- The leaves turn green.
  主语　　　系动词　表语
  叶子变绿了。

一、根据句意，完成下列句子。

1. 我爸爸是一位医生。

   My father _____ a doctor.

2. 鸡肉闻起来很香。

   The chicken _____ good.

3. 巧克力蛋糕看起来不错。

   The chocolate cake _____ nice.

4. 汤姆感到很满足。

   Tom _____ very satisfied.

5. 这双鞋很不舒服。

   The pair of shoes _____ very uncomfortable.

6. 她好像饿了。

   She _____ to be hungry.

二、判断下面的句子是否为主系表结构。是的在句子的后面打"√"，不是的打"×"。

1. Please open the window. 请把窗户打开。（ ）

2. He put two pears on the plate. 他在盘子里放了两个梨。（ ）

3. The maple leaves turn red. 枫叶变红了。（ ）

4. The green plants grow best. 绿色植物生长得最好。（ ）

5. I can get to the station on time. 我能准时到达车站。（ ）

参考答案：

一、1. is   2. smells   3. looks   4. feels   5. is   6. seems

二、1. ×   2. ×   3. √   4. √   5. ×

149

第三单元 主语 + 谓语 + 宾语

"主谓宾"结构中的动词大都由及物动词充当。要注意，及物动词后面必须接宾语才能表达完整的含义。

宾语的各个用法

1 表示动作行为的对象。

动作行为的对象是"牛奶"

· I want a glass of **milk**.
我想要一杯牛奶。

动作行为的对象是"花瓶"

· I broke the **vase** yesterday.
我昨天打碎了花瓶。

2 宾语位于及物动词或介词之后。

宾语 vegetables 放在及物动词 like 后面

· Some children don't like **vegetables**.
有些孩子不喜欢吃蔬菜。

宾语 bed 位于介词 in 之后

· We lay in **bed**.
我们躺在床上。

3 名词、代词、动词不定式、动名词、从句都可以用作宾语。

宾语 this city 是名词

· I love **this city**.
我喜欢这座城市。

宾语 him 是代词

· Your sister knew **him**.
你姐姐认识他。

宾语 to go to the park 是动词不定式

· Sam wanted **to go to the park**.
萨姆想去公园。

宾语 going swimming 是动名词词组

· My daughter likes **going swimming**.
我女儿喜欢去游泳。

4 主谓宾结构中，为了使句意表达更准确，可以使用状语。如：时间状语、地点状语、方式状语等。

时间状语

· We heard some news **yesterday**.
我们昨天听到了一些消息。

地点状语

· We eat dinner together **in the living room**.
我们一起在客厅吃晚餐。

方式状语

· I go to school **by bus**.
我坐公交车去学校。

一、圈出下列句子中的宾语。

1. A smile costs nothing. 微笑不需付出任何代价。

2. They are talking about the movie now. 他们现在正在谈论这部电影。

3. I visited my grandparents in the countryside yesterday. 我昨天去看望了我乡下的爷爷奶奶。

4. I'd like to try Thai cuisine. 我想尝试一下泰国菜。

5. Tom left his book on the table. 汤姆把书放在桌子上了。

二、结合图片，用括号中所给词的正确形式填空。

1. I _____ (buy) a lot of fruit in the mall last week.

2. We _____ (plant) trees in the park every year.

3. My mother _____ (drive) me to school every day.

4. Sue practices _____ (play) the piano every day.

5. The teacher often _____ (check) their homework.

6. Bruce _____ (live) in London a few years ago.

参考答案：

一、1. nothing 2. the movie 3. my grandparents 4. Thai cuisine 5. his book

二、1. bought 2. plant 3. drives 4. playing 5. checks 6. lived

第四单元 主语 + 谓语 + 间接宾语 + 直接宾语

有些及物动词的后面要接直接宾语和间接宾语，即"双宾语"，才能表达完整的含义。一般情况下，指人的叫间接宾语，指物的叫直接宾语。

give 给某人……　　　bring 带给某人……　　　tell 告诉某人……　　　award 授予某人……

pass 递给某人……　　send 寄给某人……　　　rent 租赁给某人……　teach 教某人……

buy 给某人买……　　leave 留给某人……　　　show 给某人看……　　write 给某人写……

直接宾语和间接宾语的位置

1 间接宾语通常放在直接宾语之前。

- My husband gives me a necklace.
  　　　　　　　　间接宾语　直接宾语

我丈夫给了我一条项链。

2 直接宾语放在间接宾语之前，有时要在间接宾语前加介词 **for**。

- I ordered a birthday cake for my daughter.
  　　　　　直接宾语　　　　间接宾语

我为女儿订了一个生日蛋糕。

book sb sth = book sth for sb
为某人预定某物
buy sb sth = buy sth for sb
为某人买某物
find sb sth = find sth for sb
为某人找到某物

3 直接宾语放在间接宾语之前，有时要在间接宾语前面加介词 **to**。

- I can lend my computer to you.
  　　　　　直接宾语　　　　间接宾语

我可以把电脑借给你。

bring sb sth = bring sth to sb
把某物带给某人
give sb sth = give sth to sb
把某物给某人
lend sb sth = lend sth to sb
把某物借给某人
write sb sth = write sth to sb
给某人写……

4 直接宾语是代词（如 it，them 等）时，只能放在间接宾语前面，且间接宾语前面要加上合适的介词。

　　it 放在间接宾语 you 的前面

- I will buy it for you.

我会给你买它的。

　　them 放在间接宾语 the classroom 的前面

- You can bring them to the classroom.

你可以把它们带到教室来。

 **Exercise**

一、请指出下列句子中的直接宾语和间接宾语。

1. My deskmate gave me some biscuits.

直接宾语：_____   间接宾语：_____

2. My mother bought a new bike for me.

直接宾语：_____   间接宾语：_____

3. Could you lend me this book?

直接宾语：_____   间接宾语：_____

4. The police told us the truth about the accident.

直接宾语：_____   间接宾语：_____

5. You should show me the passport.

直接宾语：_____   间接宾语：_____

二、写出下列句子的同义句。

1. Tom writes a letter to his father. _____

2. I booked a hotel for the manager. _____

3. My wife gave me a delicate present. _____

4. Could you find me the newspaper? _____

5. I pass the pepper to Shylock. _____

参考答案：

一、1. some biscuits; me   2. a new bike; me   3. this book; me

　　4. the truth; us   5. the passport; me

二、1. Tom writes his father a letter.

　　2. I booked the manager a hotel.

　　3. My wife gave a delicate present to me.

　　4. Could you find the newspaper for me?

　　5. I pass Shylock the pepper.

第五单元 主语 + 谓语 + 宾语 + 宾语补足语

一些及物动词的宾语之后还需要添加一个补足语才能使整个句子的含义完整。

1 名词（短语）、形容词（短语）、分词（短语）、动词不定式（短语）、介词短语等都可以充当宾语补足语。

名词 monitor 作宾语补足语

· The teacher had Tina as the **monitor**.
老师让蒂娜当班长。

形容词 handsome 作宾语补足语

· Linda thought her husband **handsome**.
琳达认为她的丈夫很英俊。

分词 flying 作宾语补足语

· I saw the bird **flying** in the sky.
我看见鸟儿在天空中飞翔。

2 有些及物动词之后接宾语时，还需要接宾语补足语来补充说明宾语的意义、状态等，这样才能表达完整的意义。我们将这类及物动词称作"不完全及物动词"。

· I **wish** you a happy trip.
祝你旅途愉快。

· The government **allowed** the public to talk about this topic.
政府允许公众谈论这个话题。

· You should **keep** the dormitory clean.
你应该保持宿舍整洁。

3 make，let，hear，watch，have 等"不完全及物动词"接动词不定式作宾语补足语时，通常省略介词 to。

· Tina **made** her son clean the room.
蒂娜让她的儿子打扫房间。

· The boss **let** his secretary book the plane ticket.
老板让他的秘书订机票。

· I **noticed** Jack play computer games.
我注意到杰克在玩电脑游戏。

常见的"不完全及物动词"有：

wish 希望	tell 告诉
notice 注意到	smell 闻到
listen to 听	start 开始
allow 允许	let 使
appoint 任命	look at 看；瞧
feel 感觉到	find 发现
get 使得	call 称
expect 预期	catch 赶上
make 使	ask 要求；请求
believe 相信	hear 听到
know 知道	see 看见
consider 认为	imagine 想象
have 使；让	think 想；认为
keep 保持	watch 注视；看
want 想要	

Exercise

一、从下面四个选项中选出最佳答案。

1. Tim always makes his little sister _____.
   A. cry   B. crying   C. to cry   D. cried

2. My mother advises us _____ there by bus.
   A. go   B. going   C. to go   D. went

3. The teacher managed to make himself _____.
   A. understand   B. understanding   C. to understand   D. understood

4. The client has kept us _____ for a long time.
   A. wait   B. waiting   C. to wait   D. waited

二、将下面错误的句子改写正确。

1. I saw Jim to enter the Internet bar just now. _____

2. My mother won't allow me to playing with dogs. _____

3. I want to know how to make this watch to work. _____

4. I will have the phone repair tomorrow. _____

5. I hear Fangfang sing in the room now. _____

6. She always makes us to laugh. _____

7. Who made you so sadly? _____

8. I heard the baby cry just now. _____

参考答案:
一、1. A   2. C   3. D   4. B
二、1. I saw Jim enter the Internet bar just now.

   2. My mother won't allow me to play with dogs.

   3. I want to know how to make this watch work.

   4. I will have the phone repaired tomorrow.

   5. I hear Fangfang singing in the room now.

   6. She always makes us laugh.

   7. Who made you so sad?

   8. I heard the baby crying just now.

第十一章

主谓一致
Subject-predicate
Consistency

第一单元 语法一致 1：谓语用单数的情况

1 主语是可数名词单数、不可数名词、单数代词、习惯用作单数名词的词。

- The house **belongs** to Mrs. Green.
  这房子是格林太太的。
- This **is** Jenny's mother.
  这是珍妮的妈妈。
- Time **is** life.
  时间就是生命。

2 主语是动名词或动名词短语、动词不定式或动词不定式短语、从句。

- Seeing **is** believing.
  眼见为实。
- To learn math well **is** difficult for me.
  学好数学对我来说很难。
- What he needs **is** your company.
  他需要的是你的陪伴。

3 主语是不定代词 either，neither，each，another，the other，(a) little，much 等以及 everyone，someone，something 等。

- Either of the two people **has** chance to win.
  这两个人中任何一个都有机会获胜。

- I feel that something **is** wrong.
  我觉得有点不对劲。

4 主语是表示"时间、价格、距离"的复数名词，可以看作一个整体。

- Two months **is** enough for me to prepare for the final test.
  两个月足以让我准备期末考试。
- One hundred dollars **is** acceptable for him.
  一百美元对他来说是可以接受的。
- Seventy miles **is** a long distance for me.
  七十英里对我来说是一段很长的距离。

5 主语是专有名词以及以 s 结尾的单数名词（如 news，works，physics 等）。

- Christmas **is** a reunion day in western countries.
  在西方国家，圣诞节是一个团聚的日子。
- Physics **is** the most difficult subject for him.
  对他来说，物理是最难的科目。

6 主语是 the number of ...（……的数目），a series of ...（一系列……），a kind of ...（……的一种）等，以及 many a + 单数名词，more than one + 单数名词等短语。

- The number of homeless people **has** decreased in recent years.
  近年来，无家可归者的数量有所下降。
- Many a student **has** failed the sports examination.
  许多学生没有通过体育考试。

Exercise

一、用括号中所给词的正确形式填空。

1. Three weeks _____ (be) enough for us to finish the project.

2. This computer _____ (belong) to me.

3. Either of you two _____ (have) a chance to run for president.

4. There _____ (be) something wrong with my computer.

5. The number of tourists _____ (tail) off in winter.

二、将下面错误的句子改写正确。

1. Two years have passed.

_____

2. The news make people astonished.

_____

3. A series of movies are coming out.

_____

4. To finish the work take a long time.

_____

5. The number of employees are reduced from 100 to 40.

_____

参考答案：

一、1. is   2. belongs   3. has   4. is   5. tails

二、1. Two years has passed.

   2. The news makes people astonished.

   3. A series of movies is coming out.

   4. To finish the work takes a long time.

   5. The number of employees is reduced from 100 to 40.

第二单元 语法一致 2：谓语用复数的情况

1 some，both，several，many，few，a number of 等作主语或修饰主语时。

· Some small companies **close** because of economic problems.

一些小公司因为经济问题而倒闭。

· Both of my parents **are** college teachers.

我的父母都是大学老师。

· Several options **are** open to us.

有几个选项供我们选择。

· Many basketball players **plan** to take part in the match.

许多篮球运动员计划参加这场比赛。

· A number of people **were** injured in the car accident.

许多人在这次车祸中受伤。

2 主语表示事物的总称，若指有生命的集合体，如 people，police，cattle，poultry 等，谓语动词用复数形式。

· The police **are** looking for the murderer.

警察正在寻找凶手。

· I don't care what people **think** of me.

我不在乎别人怎么看我。

· The cattle **are** grazing in the meadow.

牛群在草地上吃草。

3 主语是两个或两个以上的主语从句、动名词或动词不定式，强调两个或两个以上的概念时，谓语动词要用复数。

· Swimming and playing the guitar **are** my hobbies.

游泳和弹吉他是我的爱好。

· What the lady wants and what you give her **are** conflicting.

这位女士想要的和你给她的是不一致的。

4 主语由两部分构成，表示成双成对的名词，比如 shoes（鞋子），trousers（裤子），glasses（眼镜），gloves（手套）等。

· The new shoes **are** so beautiful.

这双新鞋真漂亮。

· The trousers **are** a bit loose for you.

这条裤子对你来说有点宽松。

> shoes（鞋子），trousers（裤子），glasses（眼镜），gloves（手套）常与 pair 连用，要注意，此时谓语动词要与 pair 保持一致。
> The pair of shoes **is** very comfortable.
> 这双鞋很舒服。

一、为下列句子勾选正确的答案。

1. Both my brothers ◯ is ◯ are doctors.

2. A number of errors ◯ is ◯ are in the essay.

3. The police ◯ search ◯ searches for a murderer in the mountain.

4. A pair of glasses of mine ◯ seem ◯ seems to be broken.

5. My gloves ◯ has ◯ have been missing for a long time.

二、从下面四个选项中选出最佳答案。

1. Some students _____ playing soccer on the playground now.
   A. is   B. are   C. was   D. were

2. Both my mother and my father _____ your phone number.
   A. know   B. knows   C. known   D. knowing

3. Linda and Cathy _____ good at drawing in the past.
   A. is   B. are   C. was   D. were

4. Reading novels _____ her hobby.
   A. is   B. are   C. being   D. were

5. The teacher and students _____ to the meeting together.
   A. come   B. comes   C. coming   D. is coming

参考答案：
一、1. are   2. are   3. search   4. seems   5. have
二、1. B   2. A   3. D   4. A   5. A

第三单元 语法一致 3：一些特殊情况

1 集体名词强调整体概念时，谓语动词用单数形式。集体名词强调个体概念时，谓语动词用复数形式。

audience	class	committee
crowd	family	

这里的 family 强调整体概念
- Our family **plans** to go camping in summer.
  我们全家计划夏天去野营。

这里的 family 强调个体概念
- Our whole family **gather** to celebrate my grandmother's birthday.
  我们全家人聚在一起庆祝我奶奶的生日。

2 and 连接的两个主语，如果指同一个人或物，谓语动词就用单数形式。如果指不同的人或物，谓语动词就用复数形式。

这个人是诗人兼作家，and 连接的是同一个人
- The poet and writer **is** my friend.
  这位诗人兼作家是我的朋友。

and 连接的是不同的人
- The director and the lead actor **were** invited to the celebration.
  导演和主演应邀参加了庆祝会。

3 主语是由 a lot of/lots of，the rest of，plenty of，the majority of 等构成的短语，谓语动词的单复数形式由短语后面名词的数决定。
- The rest of students **stay** in the classroom.
  其余的学生在教室待着。
- The majority of women **like** fashionable accessories.
  大多数女人都喜欢时尚的配饰。

4 百分数、分数后接名词、代词，如果是复数名词、代词，谓语动词用复数形式；如果单数名词、不可数名词、代词，谓语动词用单数形式。
- Seventy percent students in the class **have** been abroad.
  班上 70% 的学生出过国。
- One third of the workers **are** from China.
  三分之一的工人来自中国。

5 在倒装句中，谓语动词的数要与其后的主语保持一致。
- Here **comes** a bus.
  公交车来了。

- In front of the supermarket **stand** many people.
  超市前面站着许多人。

Exercise

一、为下列句子勾选正确的答案。

1. The whole class ○ take ○ takes part in the competition.

2. The committee ○ consist ○ consists of five members.

3. The bread and butter ○ is ○ are delicious.

4. Both the leading actor and the leading actress ○ is ○ are famous.

5. A red and round table ○ is ○ are exhibited in the shop.

6. The round table and the square table ○ was ○ were common in the living room.

7. Plenty of stores ○ stay ○ stays open during the Spring Festival.

8. The rest of boys ○ is ○ are going to the bar.

9. There ○ lie ○ lies a large lake in front of the house.

10. In ○ come ○ comes the shopkeeper.

二、将下面错误的句子改写正确。

1. Ninety percent of the workers has no thought of changing jobs.

_____

2. A series of products make people dizzying.

_____

3. What you saw and heard is not true.

_____

4. The rest of the bread are eaten by Kate.

_____

参考答案:

一、1. takes   2. consists   3. is   4. are   5. is
    6. were   7. stay   8. are   9. lies   10. comes

二、1. Ninety percent of the workers have no thought of changing jobs.

    2. A series of products makes people dizzying.

    3. What you saw and heard are not true.

    4. The rest of the bread is eaten by Kate.

163

第四单元 意义一致原则

1 主语表示时间、金钱、距离、体积、质量、面积时，如果意义强调总量就看作单数，谓语动词用单数形式。如果意义强调"有多少数量"就看作复数，谓语动词用复数形式。

强调总量

- That two years **is** the most painful time in my life.

  那两年是我一生中最痛苦的时光。

强调"有多少数量"

- Sixty seconds **are** usually regarded as one minute.

  六十秒通常视为一分钟。

如果是以数字作主语的单词或短语，可视为一个整体概念，谓语动词就用单数形式。但是表示两数相加或两数相乘，谓语动词既可以用单数形式，也可以用复数形式。

2 主语是"the + 形容词"的时候，在意义上指个人或抽象概念要视为单数，谓语动词用单数形式。但在意义上指一类人就应视为复数，谓语动词也用复数形式。

这里表示一类人

- The young **are** more energetic.

  年轻人更有活力。

这里表示个人概念

The new **is** studying hard.

新来的那个人学习很努力。

3 若 **and** 连接两个并列的单数主语，在意义上指同一个概念就视为单数，谓语动词用单数形式。除此之外，**and** 连接两个形容词用来修饰一个主语的时候，如果指的是两种不同的事物，此时应视为复数，谓语动词也用复数形式。

指同一个概念

- Rock and roll **has** a strong sense of rhythm.

  摇滚乐的节奏感很强。

指两种不同的事物

- Chinese and English histories **have** a big difference.

  中国和英国的历史有很大的不同。

4 **most，the last，the rest，the remainder** 等词作主语时，如果是表示单数意义，谓语动词用单数形式；如果是表示复数意义，谓语动词则用复数形式。

- Some students agreed to the proposal, while the rest **were** against it.

  这里表示复数意义

  一些学生同意这个建议，剩下的则是反对的。

- The previous attempts failed, and the last **was** related to their fate.

  这里表示单数意义

  之前的尝试都失败了，最后一次的尝试关系到他们的命运。

Exercise

一、从下面四个选项中选出最佳答案。

1. The poor _____ not always unhappy.

    A. is   B. was   C. are   D. were

2. The United States _____ founded in 1776.

    A. is   B. was   C. are   D. were

3. Another ten days _____ enough for me to prepare the meeting.

    A. is   B. been   C. are   D. were

4. Four years _____ passed quickly.

    A. have   B. has   C. having   D. had

5. The singer and the pianist _____ been invited to the party.

    A. have   B. has   C. having   D. had

二、将下面错误的句子改写正确。

1. The first and key word are somehow missing. _____

2. More than 30 percent of the earth's surface are land. _____

3. The actor and dancer are to attend our welcome party. _____

4. Eighty percent of the students in our class are fond of school meals, while the remainder dislikes them . _____

5. The old is cared for well by other people. _____

参考答案:

一、1. C   2. B   3. A   4. B   5. A

二、1. The first and key word is somehow missing.

    2. More than 30 percent of the earth's surface is land.

    3. The actor and dancer is to attend our welcome party./The actor and the dancer are to attend our welcome party.

    4. Eighty percent of the students in our class are fond of school meals, while the remainder dislike them.

    5. The old are cared for well by other people.

第五单元 就近原则和就远原则

就近原则

1 **由 either ... or ..., or, neither ... nor ..., not only ... but also ... 等连接两个并列主语时，谓语动词的单复数形式要与离它最近的主语保持一致。**

- Neither they nor Mary **likes** dancing.
  他们和玛丽都不喜欢跳舞。
- Not only I but also my parents **are** looking forward to meeting my aunt.
  不但我而且我父母也盼望着见到我的阿姨。
- I or Mary **has** a chance to take part in the match.
  我或玛丽有机会参加比赛。
- Either you or he **writes** this letter.
  这封信不是你写就是他写的。

2 **There be 句型中，要遵循就近原则。**

- There **is** a boy and three girls in the library.
  图书馆里有一个男孩和三个女孩。
- There **are** three girls and a boy in the library.
  图书馆里有三个女孩和一个男孩。

就远原则

在下列短语连接两个主语时，谓语动词的单复数形式要和离得远的主语保持一致。

along with 连同……一起
apart from 除……之外
as well as 和……一样
besides 除……之外（还）
except 除……外，不包括
in addition to 除……之外
rather than 宁可……也不愿
together with 和；连同

(×) The boy together with his friends go to a restaurant.

<u>谓语和离得远的主语保持一致</u>

- **The boy** together with his friends **goes** to a restaurant.
  这个男孩和他的朋友一起去了一家餐馆。

(×) Students as well as the teacher is invited to the activity.

<u>谓语和离得远的主语保持一致</u>

- **Students** as well as the teacher **are** invited to the activity.
  学生和老师都被邀请参加这次活动。

Exercise

一、为下列句子勾选正确的答案。

1. Either Mr. Wang or the students ○ **know** ○ **knows** this thing.

2. Where to get the information and how to get it ○ **have** ○ **has** been discussed.

3. There ○ **is** ○ **are** two dining halls on campus.

4. Neither Tim nor his friends ○ **was** ○ **were** interested in this novel.

5. Neither my father nor my brother ○ **like** ○ **likes** rock music.

二、结合图片，用括号中所给词的正确形式填空。

1. All the students, including boys and girls, _____ (like) the professor's speech.

2. Boys as well as girls _____ (be) willing to be volunteers.

3. Not only Jane but also her parents _____ (have) agreed to go camping.

4. The captain, as well as other players, _____ (be) excited.

5. Tony along with his parents often _____ (go) to the concerts.

6. A man with two children _____ (smile) happily.

参考答案：

一、 1. know   2. have   3. are   4. were   5. likes

二、 1. like   2. are   3. have   4. is   5. goes   6. smiles

第十二章

一般时
Simple Tense

第一单元 一般现在时的表达

构成：主语 + 动词原形 / 动词第三人称单数形式
作用：人或事物的特点，或经常性、习惯性的动作。

1 一般现在时第三人称单数形式不规则变形的单词只有一个 have/has。

第一人称单数用 have
- I have three storybooks.
  我有三本故事书。

第三人称单数用 has
- She has a good knowledge of physics.
  她很熟悉物理学。

第三人称单数用 has
- Lucas has a new toy, and he shares it with his partner.
  卢卡斯有一个新玩具，他和他的伙伴分享了这个玩具。

主语为第三人称单数形式，谓语动词要用第三人称单数形式。

2 一般现在时的标志性时间状语有 always，seldom，sometimes，never，usually，often，today 等。

- She always wears a blue coat.
  她总是穿着一件蓝色的外套。

- My brother usually stays up late at night.
  我哥哥经常晚上熬夜。
- He sometimes goes to the countryside to visit his grandma.
  他有时会去乡下看望他奶奶。

- I often go to the cinema with my friends.
  我经常和我的朋友去看电影。
- They seldom talk about their families.
  他们很少谈论家人。
- I never believe the words he said.
  我绝不相信他说的话。
- Cash payments are not popular today.
  现金支付在当今不流行。

 **Exercise**

一、找出下列句子的错误之处并改正。

1. Jenny live a happy life. _____

2. The car run 80 kilometers per hour. _____

3. My friends and I often has coffee together on Wednesday nights. _____

4. When the sun go down, it means the end of the day. _____

5. Ms. White proudly told me that her daughter could plays the violin. _____

6. The economy in my hometown grow rapidly these years. _____

7. My aunt work in a bank. _____

8. I usually washes clothes on my own on weekends. _____

二、将下列单词按照正确的顺序排序。

1. seldom boots in Betty winter wears _____

2. a upset she little looks _____

3. apples has six and she banana a _____

4. me leave at can't you home alone _____

5. lessons three on he piano weekends has _____

6. arrives bus three at minutes the stop next later _____

7. kindergarten go these to seven kids o'clock at _____

参考答案:

一、1. live → lives   2. run → runs   3. has → have   4. go → goes

  5. plays → play   6. grow → grows   7. work → works   8. washes → wash

二、1. Betty seldom wears boots in winter.

  2. She looks a little upset.

  3. She has six apples and a banana.

  4. You can't leave me alone at home.

  5. He has three piano lessons on weekends.

  6. The bus arrives at next stop three minutes later.

  7. These kids go to kindergarten at seven o'clock.

第二单元 一般现在时的用法

1 表示习惯性或经常性的动作，经常和表示频率的时间状语连用。如 **often**（经常），**always**（总是），**never**（从不）等。

- She always **sings** as playing the drum.
  她经常边唱歌边打鼓。
- We never **use** single-use plastic bags when shopping.
  我们在超市购物时从不使用一次性塑料袋。

2 表示普遍存在的客观事实或真理。

- As we all know, the earth **moves** around the sun.
  众所周知，地球围着太阳转。
- The water **freezes** at zero degrees and **boils** at 100 degrees.
  水在零摄氏度结成冰，100 摄氏度时沸腾。

3 用于名言警句中。

- Practice **makes** perfect.
  熟能生巧。
- Seeing **is** believing.
  眼见为实。

4 表示主语现在的状态、感觉、特征、能力等。

- He **looks** angry now.
  他现在看起来非常生气。
- The dish **tastes** strange.
  这道菜味道很奇怪。

5 在时间或条件状语从句中使用一般现在时可以表示将来的动作。

- When you **go** to the airport, I'll take a class.
  你去机场的时候，我就该上课了。
- If your homework **is** correct, I'll allow you to watch TV for an hour.
  如果你的作业全部正确，我会允许你看一小时的电视。

6 表示安排好、计划好的事情，多用于交通工具出行、到达的时间等。

- The show **begins** from 5:00 p.m. to 9:00 p.m. and **lasts** 4 hours.
  表演从下午 5 点到 9 点，持续 4 小时。
- The professor **arrives** at Beijing Airport by plane at 2:00 p.m.
  教授乘坐飞机将于下午 2 点抵达北京机场。

Exercise

一、请将括号内的动词以"一般现在时"填空。

1. She often _____ (sing) and _____ (dance) in her room.

2. He _____ (come) from Japan.

3. My brother _____ (start) running at seven past ten every morning.

4. It _____ (rain) quite often in summer.

5. If it _____ (be) sunny, we'll hold sports meeting.

6. Rookie parents always _____ (think) that they don't have rich experience in caring babies.

7. She _____ (play) an important role in my growth.

8. Elizabeth is a naughty girl. She sometime _____ (run) away from school without telling teachers.

二、从框内选择符合语境的单词，并用其正确的形式补全下面一段话。

teach
be
live
show
develop
have
ride
make
mork

George's Life

There __1__ four people in George's family. George __2__ chemistry at school, and he __3__ eight hours a day. He __4__ an elder sister whose name is Grace. He __5__ two years younger than his sister. They __6__ in different cities. He __7__ his bike to work every day, because it's a green way to get around. He __8__ a good habit of life. This __9__ him energetic at work every day. He __10__ positive attitude to life, and both students and teachers like him.

参考答案：

一、1. sings; dances 2. comes 3. starts 4. rains 5. is 6. think 7. plays 8. runs

二、1. are 2. teaches 3. works 4. has 5. is 6. live

   7. rides 8. develops 9. makes 10. shows

第三单元 一般现在时的句型

否定句

1 谓语中有情态动词，则在情态动词后加 **not**。

肯定句：I **could** leave without telling the landlord in advance.

我可以不提前和房东说就离开。

否定句：I **could not** leave without telling the landlord in advance.

我不能不提前和房东说就离开。

2 谓语中没有情态动词时，若含有系动词 am/is/are，直接在系动词之后用否定词 not。

肯定句：He **is** the boss of this company.

他是这家公司的老板。

否定句：He **is not** the boss of this company.

他不是这家公司的老板。

3 若谓语动词是行为动词，则借助于 **don't/doesn't**，谓语动词变回原形。

肯定句：Mr. Smith **likes** reading newspaper in the morning.

史密斯先生喜欢早上看报纸。

否定句：Mr. Smith **doesn't like** reading newspaper in the morning.

史密斯先生不喜欢早上看报纸。

疑问句

1 一般现在时的一般疑问句，其结构为 **"Do/Does + 主语 + 动词原形？" "be + 主语 + 表语？"** 或 **"情态动词 + 主语 + 动词原形？"**。

· **Does he study** in the Second Middle School?

他在第二中学上学吗？

· **Are you** an engineer?

你是一名工程师吗？

· **Can you pass** me the book on the desk?

你能给把桌子上的书递给我吗？

肯定回答：Yes，主语 + 助动词（do/does）/ be 动词 / 情态动词。

否定回答：No，主语 + 助动词（do/does）/ be 动词 / 情态动词 +not。

2 一般现在时的特殊疑问句，其结构为 **"特殊疑问词 + 一般疑问句开头 + 其他？"**。

· **How does he go** to the cinema?

他怎么去电影院？

3 特殊疑问句的回答一般要根据实际情况，可作简略回答，但当 **Why** 作为特殊疑问句的开头时，回答一定要以 **Because** 开头。

· — **Why** do they come home together after school?

为什么他们放学一起回家？

— **Because** they are neighbors.

因为他们是邻居。

Exercise

一、根据要求改写句子。

1. I like listening to music in my spare time.（用第三人称 he 改写句子）_____

2. I usually go to school <u>at 7:00</u>.（对划线部分进行提问）_____

3. He is a farmer.（变为一般疑问句）_____

4. Trains run according to the schedule.（改为否定句）_____

5. Beijing is <u>in the north of China</u>.（对划线部分进行提问）_____

二、从右边的方框中选出合适的词组，并用其合适的形式填空。

1. — What does the man usually do on Sundays?

   — He usually _____ and _____.

2. — How does the lady go to the hospital?

   — The lady _____ to the hospital.

3. — How often does the girl go to the beauty salon?

   — The girl goes to the beauty salon _____.

4. — Why does the little girl take medicine?

   — Because she _____.

5. — What does the boy want?

   — The boy wants _____.

> have a cold
> chat with the old
> a piece of birthday cake
> once a week
> drive to nursing home
> take a taxi

参考答案：

一、1. He likes listening to music in his spare time.

2. When/What time do you usually go to school?

3. Is he a farmer?

4. Trains don't run according to the schedule.

5. Where is Beijing?

二、1. drives to nursing home; chats with the old   2. takes a taxi

3. once a week   4. has a cold   5. a piece of birthday cake

第四单元 一般过去时的用法

结构：主语 + 动词过去式
作用：表示在过去某个时间里发生的动作、存在的状态或习惯性的动作，不强调对现在的影响，只说明过去。

1 表示过去某时发生的动作，常和 **this morning**（今天早上），**yesterday**（昨天）等表示过去的时间状语连用。

- She **played** the piano this morning.

  她今天早上弹了钢琴。

- He **left** the hotel three hours ago.

  他三小时前离开了酒店。

强调现在已经停止了过去的某个习惯时，用 used to do sth，表示"过去常常做某事"。

Alice **used to work** overtime until 10:00 p.m.

爱丽丝过去常常加班到晚上 10 点。

It **used to be** a restaurant.

这儿过去是一家餐馆。

2 表示过去习惯性的动作。

- She **liked** dancing when she was a kid.

  当她还是个孩子的时候，她非常喜欢跳舞。

- My father **walked** to school twenty years ago.

  我爸爸二十年前走路上学。

表示已经去世的人做的某事也要用过去时，即便客观事实也是如此。

Grandpa Andrew **passed** away two years ago. 安德鲁爷爷两年前去世了。

3 在"讲故事"的时候，一般过去时是经常用到的一种时态。

One day, a wallaby **played** on the grass. Her mother **sat** under a tree. Suddenly, a hunter **appeared**. The mother kangaroo **called** out "Baby, dangerous, come here." The wallaby **heard** the sound and quickly **slipped** into the mother kangaroo's bag. The mother kangaroo frantically **ran** forward. Eventually, they **ran** into the forest and **escaped** unscathed.

一天，一只小袋鼠在草地上玩耍。她的妈妈坐在树下。突然，一个猎人出现了。袋鼠妈妈叫到"宝贝，危险，快过来"。小袋鼠听到声音后迅速地钻进袋鼠妈妈的袋子里。袋鼠妈妈疯狂地向前奔跑。最终，他们跑进了森林里，毫发未伤地逃脱了。

4 一般过去时有时还带有某种感情色彩。

- The old lady always **showed** off her pearl necklace to others.

  这个老太太总是向其他人炫耀她的珍珠项链。

 **Exercise**

一、用括号中所给词的正确时态填空。

1. They _____ (build) the house three years ago.

2. I _____ (buy) some vegetables from the supermarket.

3. Nick _____ (write) an email to his pen pal yesterday.

4. Fortunately, we _____ (get) to the airport on time.

5. It _____ (rain) heavily last night, and many villages were _____ (destroy).

6. Tom _____ (spend) a happy weekend with his grandpa.

7. Teachers _____ (organize) us to play games in break time.

8. Dora _____ (study) hard and she finally _____ (pass) the Politics examination.

9. The little girl _____ (be) happy, because she _____ (receive) a new dress.

10. Linda _____ (be) so tired that she _____ (go) to bed earlier today.

二、从下列选项中选出一个最佳选项。

1. — Where did you go these days?

   — I _____ the Great Wall with my family.

   A. walked   B. go   C. went to   D. visit

2. Mike _____ his driver's license last year.

   A. get   B. gets   C. got   D. will got

3. I _____ a rainbow after the storm.

   A. see   B. seeing   C. sees   D. saw

4. He didn't _____ home and _____ at a hotel last night.

   A. go; stay   B. goes; stays   C. went; stayed   D. go; stayed

5. She _____ an appointment with Alice yesterday.

   A. make   B. makes   C. made   D. making

参考答案：

一、1. built   2. bought   3. wrote   4. got   5. rained; destroyed   6. spent

　　7. organized   8. studied; passed   9. was; received   10. was; went

二、1. C   2. C   3. D   4. D   5. C

第五单元 一般过去时的句型

否定句

1 如果句中含有 **was/were**，要在后面 **+ not**。

肯定句：He **was** the last one to come in.
他是最后一个进来的人。

否定句：He **wasn't** the last one to come in.
他不是最后一个进来的人。

肯定句：They **were** smart when they were young.
他们小的时候很聪明。

否定句：They **were not** smart when they were young.
他们小的时候并不聪明。

2 如果句中的谓语动词是实义动词，要在前面加上 **didn't**，并将动词的过去式改为原形。

肯定句：We **went** to the zoo last weekend.
我们上周末去了动物园。

否定句：We **didn't go** to the zoo last weekend.
我们上周末没有去动物园。

肯定句：They **invited** Bob to the party.
他们邀请鲍勃参加派对。

否定句：They **didn't invite** Bob to the party.
他们没有邀请鲍勃参加派对。

疑问句

1 如果句中含有 **was/were**，则将其提前。

• She was a dancer before. ——提前
Was she a dancer before?
她之前是一名舞者吗？

• They were satisfied with the product this time. ——提前
Were they satisfied with the product this time?
他们对这次的产品满意吗？

2 如果句中的谓语动词是实义动词，则把助动词 **did** 放在句首，句中的实义动词用原形。

• He forgot to close the window before leaving yesterday. ——变为原形
Did he forget to close the window before leaving yesterday?
他在昨天走之前忘记关窗户了吗？

• You finished the task on time. ——变为原形
Did you finish the task on time?
你按时完成任务了吗？

3 一般过去时的特殊疑问句结构为"特殊疑问词 + 一般疑问句开头 + 其他？"。

• **Why** did you give her an umbrella?
你为什么给她一把伞？

• **When** did you arrive at the train station?
你什么时候到达火车站？

• **Where** did you go last night?
你昨天晚上去哪儿了？

Exercise

一、找出下列句子中的错误并改正。

1. They leave some money on the table yesterday. _____

2. Workers detect a batch of substandard products last month. _____

3. The boss owes the employee two months' salary last year. _____

4. She spend all her savings in treating her illness when she was thirty. _____

5. The editor do not find all the proofing errors last time. _____

6. The rich man receives a threatening letter today. _____

7. He make up himself and manage to fool the police. _____

8. Eden escape from a car accident just now. _____

9. I hand my resignation to my leader last week. _____

10. The couple were used to live in Manchester City. _____

二、根据要求改写句子。

1. They graduated from university this summer. (改为一般疑问句)

_____

2. The kind lady adopted the poor girl. (改为否定句)

_____

3. His company went bankrupt last winter. (对划线部分进行提问)

_____

4. David went fishing by the river last week. (改为否定句)

_____

参考答案：

一、1. leave → left 2. detect → detected 3. own → owed 4. spend → spent
    5. do → did 6. receive → received 7. make → made；manage → managed
    8. escape → escaped 9. hand → handed 10. 去掉 were

二、1. Did they graduate from university this summer?
    2. The kind lady didn't adopt the poor girl.
    3. When did his company go bankrupt?
    4. David didn't go fishing by the river last week.

第十三章

将来时
Future Tense

第一单元 一般将来时的用法

1 表示将要发生的动作。

常常和 tomorrow（明天），after ten days（十天之后）等表示将来的时间状语连用。一般将来时的句子构成为"be going to do"或"will/shall do"。

表示十天后要做的事
- He **will quit** after ten days.

  他将在十天后辞职。

表示一个月后要做的事
- I'm **going to** move next month.

  我下个月要搬家了。

2 表示意愿。

表示意愿
- I **will encourage** you if you take part in the contest.

  如果你参加比赛，我会鼓励你的。

表示意愿
- I **will play** with you if you come here.

  如果你来这里，我会和你一起玩。

3 "am/is/are + to + 动词原形"表示按计划要发生的动作。

表示按计划要做的事
- He **is to retire** at the age of sixty.

  他要在 60 岁时退休。

4 "am/is/are + about to + 动词原形"表示"马上"。

表示马上要出发
- The train **is about to** set out.

  火车就要出发了。

表示马上要去图书馆
- We **are about to** go to the library together.

  我们正要一起去图书馆。

表示马上要展示
- I **am about to** show you how to use it.

  我将向你展示如何使用它。

5 "in + 一段时间"表示从说话人说话的时刻为起点的"一段时间后"，用于一般将来时。

表示十分钟后到达
- The plane will arrive **in ten minutes**.

  飞机将在十分钟后到达。

表示两分钟后到达
- I'll reach the office **in two minutes**.

  我将在两分钟后到办公室。

6 在"祈使句 + and/or + 句子"结构中，and/or 后面的句子要用将来时。

祈使句 + or + 句子，句子用将来时
- Hurry up, or you **will** be late for work.

  快点，不然你上班就要迟到了。

祈使句 + and + 句子，句子用将来时
- Walk along the street, and you **will** find the drugstore.
- 沿着这条街走，你就会找到药店。

Exercise

一、用括号中所给词的正确时态填空。

1. I _____ (go) to Shanghai next week.

2. We are _____ (go) to meet at five o'clock.

3. He will _____ (teach) us math next year.

4. Tomorrow _____ (be) Saturday.

5. It's _____ (snow) tomorrow.

6. Jenny _____ (go) hiking with us if the weather is fine.

7. I _____ (take) part in the camp next summer.

8. This machine _____ (play) an important role in the future.

9. I _____ (visit) the museum with my parents tomorrow.

10. The cinema _____ (close) in two hours.

二、请从下面方框中选择合适的单词，用其正确的形式补全下面一段话。

make   drive   be   hold   buy

Tomorrow is my grandpa's birthday. We __1__ a big birthday party for him. My father __2__ us there. He will buy a new coat for my grandpa. My mother will buy a birthday cake. I __3__ a card by hand. We __4__ a lot of vegetables and fruit to prepare today. I'm looking forward to the party. I am sure grandpa __5__ very happy.

参考答案：

一、1. will go   2. going   3. teach   4. is   5. going to snow

6. will go   7. will take   8. will play   9. will visit   10. will be closed

二、1. will hold   2. will drive   3. will make   4. bought   5. will be

第二单元 一般将来时的句型

疑问句

1 以 **will/shall** 开头的疑问句表示请求或意愿时，**shall** 用于第一人称，**will** 用于第二人称。

will 用于第二人称
- **Will you** please close the window?
  请你把窗户关上好吗？

shall 用于第一人称
- **Shall we** go to the art gallery?
  我们去美术馆好吗？

shall 用于第一人称
- **Shall I** go to the museum with you?
  我和你一起去博物馆好吗？

2 一般疑问句：把 **will/am/is/are** 提至句首。

把 will 放到句首
- **Will** you be home tomorrow?
  你明天会到家吗？

把 be 动词放到句首
- **Are** you going to see the ball game with me?
  你要和我一起去看球赛吗？

3 特殊疑问句：一般将来时的特殊疑问句结构为"特殊疑问词 + 一般疑问句开头 + 其他？"。

特殊疑问词
- **What** are you going to do on vacation?
  be 动词提前，为一般疑问句
  你假期打算做什么？

特殊疑问词
- **What** will you do after school?
  will 提前，为一般疑问句
  放学后你要做什么？

否定句

如果句中含有 **am/is/are**，要在后面 **+ not**。如果句中的谓语动词是"**will + 实义动词**"，要在 **will** 后面 **+ not**。

肯定句：She **is** going to take part in the match.
她打算参加比赛。

在 be 动词后加 not
否定句：She **is not** going to take part in the match.
她不打算参加比赛。

肯定句：Her opinion **will** affect my decision.
她的意见会影响我的决定。

在 will 后加 not
否定句：Her opinion **will not** affect my decision.
她的意见不会影响我的决定。

Exercise

一、根据要求改写句子。

1. I'm going to the hospital tomorrow. （改为否定句） _____

2. I'll send you the birthday gift.（改为否定句） _____

3. You are going to visit your grandmother. （改为疑问句） _____

4. He will have a meeting. （改为疑问句） _____

5. We shall have the set menu. （改为疑问句） _____

二、从下面方框中选择合适的动词填空，句子要用一般将来时。

| go open take finish meet hurt |

1. I _____ my homework before going home.

2. Will you please _____ the window?

3. It _____ me a lot of time to study English well.

4. My parents _____ to church this Saturday.

5. Don't eat ice cream, or your stomach _____.

6. I am going _____ him at the gate.

参考答案：

一、1. I'm not going to the hospital tomorrow.   2. I won't send you the birthday gift.

　　3. Are you going to visit your grandmother?   4. Will he have a meeting?

　　5. Shall we have the set menu?

二、1. will finish   2. open   3. will take   4. will go   5. will hurt   6. to meet

第三单元 will 和 be going to 的区别

1 和 **be going to** 相比，**will** 与现在的时间相隔较远。

不是马上去

· I **will** go to the supermarket with my mother.

我会和我的妈妈一起去超市。

马上就要去

· I **am going to** go to the supermarket with my mother.

我要和我的妈妈一起去超市。

2 **be going to** 有"计划，准备"等含义，而 **will** 没有这层含义。

表示计划要做的事

· I **am going to** stop gambling.

我打算戒赌了。

· I **will** stop gambling.

我会戒赌的。

3 **be going to** 偏向主观上要做某事，**will** 是客观上会发生某事。

表示主观上要去做

· I **am going to** ask Tom for help.

我打算向汤姆寻求帮助。

表示客观上会发生的事

· Summer **will** come next month.

下个月夏天就要来了。

4 在包含条件从句的主句中，一般使用 **will**。

主句有条件状语，使用 will

· If you come with me, I **will** invite you for dinner.

如果你和我一块去，我就请你吃饭。

（×）If you come with me, I **am going to** invite you for dinner.

如果你和我一块去，我就请你吃饭。

Exercise

一、为下列句子勾选正确的答案。

1. We ○ **are going to** ○ **will** see a doctor in ten minutes.

2. The weather report says it ○ **is going to** ○ **will** snow tomorrow.

3. I'm seriously ill. I ○ **am going to** ○ **will** die.

4. If I have time, I ○ **am going to** ○ **will** play all the time.

5. I ○ **am going to** ○ **will** earn a lot of money one day.

二、请从下面方框中选择合适的动词，搭配 **will** 或 **be going to** 完成句子。

rent   go   have   take

1. I _____ a glass of wine.

2. I _____ a house with my family.

3. I _____ these clothes of my family.

4. If you leave it up to me, I _____ to the cinema.

参考答案：

一、1. are going to   2. will   3. am going to   4. will   5. will

二、1. will have   2. am going to rent   3. am going to wash   4. will go

第四单元 过去将来时的用法

1 表示从过去某一时间来看将要发生的动作。一般形式是 **"should/would + 动词原形"** 或 **"was/were + going to + 动词原形"**。

> 表示从昨天来看明年要发生的动作

- Yesterday, she said she **would graduate** from high school next year.

  昨天，她说她明年将从高中毕业。

> 表示从过去来看十分钟后要发生的动作

- He just said that he **would go** home in ten minutes.

  他刚刚说十分钟后回家。

2 某些具有短暂性动作含义的动词用过去进行时可以表示过去将来时，如 **come，leave，start，stay** 等。这些词在句中表示过去将来时的结构为 **"was/were + 动词 ing 形式"**。

> 用过去进行时表示过去将来时

- I told Tina the plane **was arriving** in one hour. *瞬间动词*

  我告诉过蒂娜，飞机会在一小时内到。

3 **"was/were + to + 动词原形"** 表示过去按计划要发生的动作。

> 表示过去按计划要做的事

- She **was to** go out to buy some fruit.

  她要出去买一些水果。

- They **were to** meet at the school gate.

  他们打算在校门口见面。

4 **"was/were + about to + 动词原形"** 表示从过去某一时间来看的"马上"。

> 表示从过去来看的"马上"

- I **was about to** tell you the truth.

  我正要告诉你真相。

- We **were about to** leave when someone knocked at the door.

  我们正要离开时，有人敲门。

Exercise

一、找出下列句子的错误之处并改正。

1. Tom said he spent his holiday next year. _____

2. She said she resigned the next day. _____

3. I hoped that you would come to my party tomorrow. _____

4. Mother said she took me to Disneyland in summer holiday. _____

5. I was not sure whether they went to buy books. _____

二、请将括号内的动词以"过去将来时"填空。

1. Tina said she _____ (visit) the Palace Museum next summer.

2. I told you that I _____ (not stay) here for a long time.

3. I was not sure whether my father _____ (go) home the next year.

4. Tom told me the bus _____ (come) in ten minutes.

5. Lily said she _____ (be) happy if I came to visit her.

6. I said they _____ (be come) friends quickly.

参考答案：

一、 1. spent → would spend   2. resigned → would resign   3. would come → were coming

　　 4. took → would take   5. went → were going

二、 1. would visit   2. would not stay   3. would go

　　 4. was coming   5. would be   6. would become

第十四章

进行时
Continuous Tense

第一单元 现在进行时的用法

构成 am/is/are + 动词 ing 形式

- I am doing my homework.
  我正在做作业。
- She is cleaning the room.
  她正在打扫房间。
- They are playing basketball.
  他们正在打篮球。

1 表示正在进行的动作，可与 now，right now，at this moment 等表示现在的时间状语连用。

- I **am drinking** soybean milk <u>now</u>.
  我现在在喝豆浆。
- They **are practicing** the Christmas carol <u>right now</u>.
  他们现在正在练习唱圣诞颂歌。
- She **is traveling** in the United States <u>at this moment</u>.
  她现在正在美国旅行。

2 表示现阶段一直在进行的动作。

- I **am preparing** for the competition these days.
  我这几天一直在为竞赛做准备。
- I **am learning** to swim for these months.
  这几个月我在学游泳。
- I'm **writing** the thesis these days.
  这些天我一直在写论文。

3 某些具有短暂性动作含义的动词用现在进行时可以表示将来。如 **come**，**leave**，**start**，**stay**，**go**，**fly**，**walk** 等。

- I **am staying** here for a day.
  我要在这里待一天。
- He **is going** home tomorrow.
  他明天要回家了。
- The tour group **is arriving** at the hotel in two hours.
  旅游团将在两小时内到达酒店。
- Our company **is starting** the project at the end of this month.
  我们公司要在月底开启这个项目。
- I **am flying** to Janpan on business next week.
  我下周要乘飞机去日本出差。

4 有些介词短语作表语时，可以表示正在进行时。

- The urgent project is **under discussion**.
  这个紧急项目正在讨论中。
- Don't bother me. I am **at work** now.
  别打扰我，我现在正在工作。

Exercise

一、请将括号内的动词以"现在进行时"的形式填空。

1. He _____ (fly) to Japan on business.

2. They _____ (play) soccer in the playground now.

3. Look! She _____ (sing) a song.

4. The students _____ (swim) in the pool.

5. I _____ (teach) math in a high school these years.

二、根据图片提示，用"现在进行时"回答下面问题。

— What are you doing in the room?

— _____

— What is he doing in the kitchen?

— _____

— What's your mother doing?

— _____

— What is she doing in the mall?

— _____

参考答案：

一、1. is flying   2. are playing   3. is singing   4. are swimming   5. am teaching

二、1. I am reading a book.   2. He is cleaning the kitchen.

　　3. She is washing the fruit.   4. She is shopping with her son.

第二单元 一般现在时和现在进行时的区别

比较：

一般现在时	现在进行时
Do you often cook at home?	Are you cooking at home now?
你经常在家做饭吗？	你现在在家做饭吗？

1 一般现在时用来表示习惯性的动作。

表示习惯性的动作
- I usually **take** a walk in the park.

  我通常在公园里散步。

表示习惯性的动作
- I **like** eating dumplings in this restaurant.

  我喜欢吃这家餐厅的饺子。

现在进行时表示正在进行或发生的动作。

表示正在进行的动作
- I **am taking** a walk in the park now.

  我正在公园里散步。

表示正在发生的动作
- I **am eating** dumplings. They're so delicious.

  我正在吃饺子。它们如此美味。

2 一般现在时是用来表示长时间维持不变的情况。

表示每年夏天都去
- She **goes to** the nursing home every summer.

  她每年夏天都去养老院。

表示每天早上都在家吃早餐
- I always **have breakfast** at home.

  我总是在家里吃早餐。

现在进行时用来表示目前暂时发生的情况。

表示目前暂时在写论文
- She **is writing** her paper in the library.

  她正在图书馆写论文。

表示现在在家吃早餐
- I **am having** breakfast at home now.

  我现在正在家里吃早餐。

3 一般现在时往往不带任何感情色彩。

- It often **rains** in summer.

  夏天经常下雨。

- Tim **drives** too fast on the road.

  蒂姆在路上开得太快了。

现在进行时与 **always**，**forever** 等词连用表示一直、反复出现的动作，常常表现出说话者的某种情绪。

- It **is always raining** in summer. I don't like it.

  夏天总是下雨，我很不喜欢。

- Tim **is always driving** too fast on the road. It's so dangerous.

  蒂姆总是在路上开得太快，太危险了。

Exercise

一、为下列句子勾选正确的答案。

1. I ○ am getting ○ get up at seven o'clock every morning.

2. She ○ is looking ○ looks for a new job now.

3. The earth ○ is getting ○ goes around the sun.

4. What a mess! You are always ○ throwing ○ throw things around.

5. I ○ am feeding ○ feed the cat at this moment.

二、请以括号内动词的 "一般现在时" 或 "现在进行时" 形式填空。

1. My parents _____ (read) newspapers every morning.

2. I _____ (take) a walk with my husband together in the evening.

3. My son _____ (fly) a kite in the garden now.

4. I _____ (go) to the hospital now.

5. The man _____ (teach) us to draw on Sundays.

参考答案：
一、1. get　2. is looking　3. goes　4. throwing　5. am feeding
二、1. read　2. take　3. is flying　4. am going　5. teaches

第三单元 过去进行时的用法

构成 was/were + 动词 ing 形式

· I was celebrating my birthday when you called.

你打电话来的时候我正在庆祝生日。

· They were playing in the yard together.

他们正一起在院子里玩。

1 表示过去某一时刻或某段时间正在发生的某事。可与 at that time，this time yesterday，the whole morning 等时间状语连用。

· Mark was doing his homework at this time yesterday.

马克昨天这个时候正在写作业。

· I was cooking when my father got home.

父亲到家的时候我正在做饭。

· She was speaking in the hall the whole morning.

她整个上午都在礼堂里演讲。

2 "was/were + 动词 ing 形式" 与 always，forever 等词连用时，表示过去一直、反复出现的动作，常常表现出说话者的某种情绪。

表现了说话者疑惑、厌烦的情绪

· He was always wearing the same clothes.

他（过去）总是穿同样的衣服。

表现了说话者不满的情绪

· He was always going out without turning off the light.

他（过去）经常不关灯就出去。

3 "was/were + 动词 ing 形式" 结构有时不表示过去正在发生的事情，而表示过去某个时间按计划、安排等将要发生的动作。

· He told me he was going to Beijing last night.

他昨晚告诉我他马上要去北京了。

· Yesterday, I heard that Tom was going abroad.

昨天，我听说汤姆要出国了。

4 过去进行时用于宾语从句、时间状语从句时，表示与主句的动作同时进行，此时句中通常没有时间状语。

· She was still working when I was on my way home.

我在回家的路上时，她还在工作。

· Christine was playing computer games while Bella was doing homework.

克里斯汀在玩电脑游戏，而贝拉在做作业。

when 和 while 都可以表示"当……的时候"，when 既可以表示时间点，也可表示一段时间，while 只能表示一段时间。因此 when 引导的从句中的谓语动词既能是瞬间动词，也能是延续性动词，而 while 引导的从句中的谓语动词必须是延续性动词。

I was writing a letter when the teacher came in.

老师进来的时候，我正在写信。

He was listening to music when/while I was sleeping.

我在睡觉的时候，他在听音乐。

Exercise

一、将下面错误的句子改写正确。

1. I slept at this time yesterday. _____

2. We had dinner when the doorbell rang. _____

3. What were you do at ten o'clock yesterday? _____

4. I was cooking when he is cleaning the car. _____

5. I watched TV at this time yesterday. _____

二、读下列对话，并用正确的时态填空。

1. — Why didn't you call me back?
   — Sorry, I _____ (call) my mother at that time.

2. — Why weren't you at home just now?
   — I _____ (shop) with my mother at that time.

3. — You look unhappy. What happened?
   — Carol was always _____ (talk) with me in the class.

参考答案：

一、1. I was sleeping at this time yesterday.

2. We were having dinner when the doorbell rang.

3. What were you doing at ten o'clock yesterday?

4. I was cooking when he was cleaning the car.

5. I was watching TV at this time yesterday.

二、1. was calling 2. was shopping 3. talking

197

第四单元 进行时的疑问句和否定句

现在进行时的疑问句和否定句

➔ 一般疑问句：把 am/is/are 提前至句首。

- My father is cooking in the kitchen.
  我爸爸正在厨房做饭。——把 is 提到句首
- Is your father cooking in the kitchen?
  你爸爸在厨房做饭吗？

➔ 特殊疑问句：特殊疑问词 + 一般疑问句开头 + 其他？

特殊疑问词
- Why are you talking about this?
  你为什么要讨论这个？

➔ 否定形式：只需在 am/is/are 后面 + not。

- They are watching the news.
  他们正在看新闻。——在 are 后加 not
- They are not watching the news.
  他们没有在看新闻。

过去进行时的疑问句和否定句

➔ 一般疑问句：把 was/were 提前至句首。

- He was having dinner ten minutes ago.
  他十分钟前在吃晚餐。——把 was 提到句首
- Was he having dinner ten minutes ago?
  十分钟前他在吃晚餐吗？

➔ 特殊疑问句形式：特殊疑问词 + 一般疑问句开头 + 其他？

特殊疑问词
- What were you doing at this time yesterday?
  昨天这个时候你在干什么？

➔ 否定形式：在 was/were 后面 + not。

- I was reading a novel at nine o'clock.
  九点钟的时候我正在看小说。——在 was 后加 not
- I was not reading a novel at nine o'clock.
  九点钟的时候我没在看小说。

 **Exercise**

一、根据要求改写句子。

1. We are making models these days. （改为否定句）
_____

2. They are playing the guitar now. （改为一般疑问句）
_____

3. He is reviewing lessons in his room. （改为一般疑问句）
_____

4. I was repairing my bike. （改为否定句）
_____

5. Tom was reading books at this time yesterday. （对划线部分进行提问）
_____

二、用括号中所给词的正确时态填空。

1. Jack _____ (watch) TV at this time yesterday.

2. Linda _____ (play) games in her bedroom now.

3. We _____ (sleep) when the phone rang.

4. Listen! Our manager _____ (sing) a popular song.

5. When I _____ (do) my homework, the light went out.

参考答案：

一、1. We are not making models these days.

2. Are they playing the guitar now?

3. Is he reviewing lessons in his room?

4. I wasn't repairing my bike.

5. What was Tom doing at this time yesterday?

二、1. was watching   2. is playing   3. were sleeping   4. is singing   5. was doing

第五单元 不能用于进行时的动词

1 表示爱憎的动词

like	love
prefer	adore
dislike	hate
mind	object

(×) I am liking eating chocolate.

(√) I **like** eating chocolate.

我喜欢吃巧克力。

2 表达希望和意愿的动词

want	desire
agree	wish
hope	expect

(×) I am hoping you can come back soon.

(√) I **hope** you can come back soon.

我希望你能尽快回来。

3 表达知道、相信、猜想的动词

know	believe
think	suppose
wonder	doubt

(×) She is doubting the truth of the matter.

(√) She **doubts** the truth of the matter.

她怀疑这件事的真实性。

4 表达无法持续的动作

accept	admit
allow	decide
deny	die
end	exist
need	permit
promise	refuse

(×) I am refusing to compromise on this matter.

(√) I **refuse** to compromise on this matter.

我拒绝在这件事上妥协。

5 表示感觉、感官的动词

see	hear
smell	taste
feel	

(×) The cake is tasting sweet.

(√) The cake **tastes** sweet.

这蛋糕尝起来很甜。

Exercise

一、为下列句子勾选正确的答案。

1. ○ Are you believing ○ Do you believe what he says?

2. She ○ is not liking ○ doesn't like bright colors.

3. This bag ○ belongs ○ is belonging to Scott.

4. Jean ○ was hearing ○ heard the good news.

5. He ○ is not needing ○ doesn't need more food.

二、从下面方框中选择合适的动词填空，注意句子的时态。

> see   buy   cost   listen

1. The coat _____ me 500 dollars.

2. Be quiet. I _____ to music now.

3. When I was at my friend's house, I _____ a new album.

4. My father _____ a new car.

参考答案：

一、1. Do you believe   2. doesn't like   3. belongs   4. heard   5. doesn't need

二、1. cost   2. am listening   3. saw   4. bought

第十五章

完成时
Perfect Tense

第一单元 现在完成时的用法

构成

I/you/we/they + have done

I've/you've/we've/they've + done

he/she/it + has done

he's/she's/it's + done

- I **have prepared** my meal.

  我已经做好饭了。

- We**'ve finished** reading this book.

  我们已经看完了这本书。

- He **has given** up smoking.

  他已经戒烟了。

- She**'s had** the scar removed.

  她已经把伤疤去掉了。

1 表示过去发生并完成、对现在仍有影响的动作。

- I **have fulfilled** my promise to you.

  我已经履行了对你的承诺。

- He **has divorced** with his wife.

  他已经和妻子离婚了。

2 现在完成时常和某些标志性词语连用，这些标志性词语有：**already** 已经，**yet** 已经，**since...** 自从，**for...**，**recently** 最近，**lately** 近来，**so far** 迄今为止等。

- They **have** already **grown** up.

  他们已经长大了。

- What **have** you **found** so far?

  到目前为止，你发现了什么？

3 表示过去的动作一直持续到现在，甚至有可能继续持续下去。表示此含义时常和某些词连用，这些标志性词语有：**for +** 一段时间，**since +** 时间点或从句等。

可能还会继续在这家小公司工作

- Jesse **has worked** in this small company for ten years.

  杰西在这家小公司工作了十年。

可能还会继续在这里住下去

- We **have lived** in the old house since 1998.

  我们从 1998 年起就一直住在这座老房子里。

4 现在完成时与 **ever**，**never** 等表示频率的时间副词连用。

- Have you **ever** been to Spain?

  你去过西班牙吗？

- I have **never** been to Singapore.

  我从未去过新加坡。

5 **have/has been to** 表示去过某地，现在已经回来了；**have/has gone to** 表示去了某地，现在还没回来。

去过伦敦，现在已经回来了

- I **have been to** London once.

  我去过伦敦一次。

去了澳大利亚，还没回来

- Leo **has gone to** Australia for work.

  利奥去澳大利亚工作了。

 **Exercise**

一、用括号中所给词的正确时态填空。

1. I _____ (write) three novels since 2018.

2. The hamburgers _____ (arrive). Let's enjoy them.

3. I _____ (learn) to play the piano since I was seven.

4. Helen _____ (work) in the hospital for three years.

5. I _____ (own) a car for several months.

6. I _____ (live) in this town since five years ago.

7. The new building _____ (build) for one month.

8. He _____ (stop) smoking. The cigarettes are not his.

9. I _____ (read) ten books so far.

10. My brother _____ (be) in the army for four years.

二、将下面错误的句子改写正确。

1. How long are you working on this project? _____

2. I never seen her before. _____

3. He has been to visit his parents and will be back soon. _____

4. I have this milk tea twice. _____

5. I already had lunch. I am full. _____

参考答案：

一、1. have written   2. have arrived   3. have learned   4. has worked   5. have owned
   6. have lived   7. has been built   8. has stopped   9. have read   10. has been

二、1. How long have you worked on this project?
   2. I have never seen her before.
   3. He has gone to visit his parents and will be back soon.
   4. I have had this milk tea twice.
   5. I have already had lunch. I am full.

第二单元 现在完成时和一般过去时的区别

区别

1 现在完成时与一般过去时都可以表示某动作结束于过去。一般过去时只表示动作的结束；现在完成时表示已结束的动作对现在造成了影响。试比较：

> 表示昨天看完了电影

- I **watched** this movie yesterday.
  我昨天看的这部电影。

> 表示已经结束的动作，对现在造成了影响

- I **have watched** this movie. I don't want to watch it again.
  我已经看过这部电影了。我不想再看一遍了。

2 现在完成时表示持续性动作时，常使用延续性动词而非瞬间动词。一般过去时则都可用。试比较：

> buy 是瞬间动词

- My mother **bought** a beautiful dress for me.
  我妈妈给我买了一条漂亮的连衣裙。

> live 是延续性动词

- Lily **lived** in the countryside in the past.
  莉莉过去住在乡下。

> study 是延续性动词

- Lily **has studied** abroad for four years.
  莉莉在国外学习了四年。

瞬间动词和延续性动词

瞬间动词表示短暂性、一次性的动作	go 去	give 给	come 来	fall 落下
	borrow 借	happen 发生	become 成为	finish 结束
	arrive 到达	leave 离开	die 死	lose 丢失
延续性动词又叫持续性动词。它指的是能够延续的动作，这种动作可以长时间延续下去或产生持久的影响	work 工作	study 学习	lie 躺	live 生活
	wait 等待	wear 穿	stand 站	sit 坐
	consider 思考	sleep 睡觉	rain 下雨	stay 停留

1 瞬间动词并不是完全不能用于完成时表示持续性的动作，它可以用于否定结构的完成时。

> see 是瞬间动词，用于否定结构的完成时中

- I **haven't seen** my daughter for one year.
  我已经一年没见我女儿了。

2 如果句子中需要使用瞬间动词来表示延续性动作，有以下两种情况：

◎ 把瞬间动词换为可以表示延续性动作的词。

put on → wear　　come → be here
fall asleep → be asleep

◎ 或者使用句型替代：**It has been +** 时间 **+ since +** 主语 **+** 谓语（**+** 其他成分）**+** 表示过去的时间状语。

- **It has been** ten years **since** we met last time.
  自我们上次见面以来，已经过去十年了。

 **Exercise**

一、用括号中所给词的正确时态填空。

1. I _____ already _____ (write) a letter to the neighbor.

2. He _____ (leave) the company two hours ago.

3. My parents _____ (come) back two weeks ago.

4. My family _____ (buy) the new house one year ago.

5. I _____ (not lend) him money last time.

6. I _____ (catch) my cat in the park this morning.

7. So far this year, many companies _____ (fail).

8. I _____ never _____ (travel) by air before.

二、为下列句子勾选正确的答案。

1. Mr. Black ○ has lived ○ lived there for four years.

2. We ○ have planted ○ planted over 200 trees here yesterday.

3. So far we ○ have planted ○ planted over 200 trees here.

4. I ○ have seen ○ saw the film *Avatar* already.

5. It ○ has snowed ○ snowed for two days.

6. I ○ have been ○ went to the National Park last week.

7. She ○ has kept ○ kept my computer for two years.

8. She ○ has read ○ read this magazine just now.

9. I ○ have bought ○ bought this phone two years ago.

10. I ○ have been invited ○ was invited to the party yesterday.

参考答案：

一、1. have; written 2. left 3. came 4. bought 5. didn't lend

　　6. caught 7. have failed 8. have; traveled

二、1. has lived 2. planted 3. have planted 4. have seen 5. has snowed

　　6. went 7. has kept 8. read 9. bought 10. was invited

第三单元 过去完成时的用法

构成 "助动词 **had** + 动词的过去分词"

· I **hadn't seen** her after I graduated from high school.

高中毕业以后，我就没见过她了。

· She **had left** when the cinema closed.

当电影院关门时，她已经离开了。

1 表示在过去某一时间之前已经完成的动作，即该动作发生在"过去的过去"。

"飞机起飞"发生在"我们到达"之前

· The plane **had taken off** before we **arrived**.

"我们到达"这件事，发生在过去。

我们到达之前飞机已经起飞了。

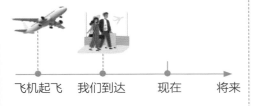

| 飞机起飞 | 我们到达 | 现在 | 将来 |

2 过去完成时常和某些时间状语连用，如：**by**，**by the end of** + 一段时间，**already**，**since**，**for** + 一段时间等。

· I **had** already **finished** my homework before my father went home.

在父亲回家之前，我已经写完了作业。

· The meeting **had been over** by the time you got there.

等你到那里的时候，会议已经结束了。

3 表示从过去某一时间开始的动作一直持续到过去的另一时间。此时常和 **since**，**for** 等引导的时间状语连用。

· She said she **hadn't spoken** to her husband since 2020.

她说自从 2020 年开始，她就不再和丈夫说话了。

4 有些表示愿望、希望、想法、意图的词可以通过使用过去完成时来表示这些事情没有实现。这些词有 **hope**，**wish**，**expect**，**plan** 等。

用过去完成时表示看电影没有实现

· He **had hoped** to go to the cinema, but he missed it because of weather.

他本希望去看电影，但由于天气原因没去。

用过去完成时表示收拾东西没有做到

· I **had meant** to have cleaned up the things before you came.

我打算在你来之前就把东西都收拾干净的。

5 如果动词的过去式 **told**，**said**，**heard**，**knew**，**thought** 等出现在宾语从句或间接引语中，发生在这些动词之前的动作要用过去完成时。

· She said she **had read** this letter.

她说她已经看过这封信了。

· I knew she **had passed** the test.

我知道她已经通过考试了。

Exercise

一、用括号中所给词的正确时态填空。

1. We _____ (decorate) the house before we moved in.

2. She _____ (finish) reading the novel by ten o'clock yesterday morning.

3. We _____ (learn) about two thousand English words by the end of last year.

4. I _____ (turn) off the alarm clock before I got up.

5. The workers _____ (plant) a lot of trees before last year.

二、从下面方框中选择合适的动词填空，句子要用"过去完成时"。

collect   read   have   stop

1. She said that she _____ the novel before.

2. When I went out, the snow _____.

3. Peter _____ many stamps before he was ten.

4. They _____ breakfast before they arrived at school.

参考答案：

一、1. had decorated   2. had finished   3. had learned   4. had turned   5. had planted

二、1. had read   2. had stopped   3. had collected   4. had had

第四单元 必须用过去完成时的句型

It was the + 序数词 + time + that 从句（从句要用过去完成时）

- It was the first time that I **had visited** the Imperial Palace.

  这是我第一次去故宫。

- It was the third time that I **had lost** my phone.

  这是我第三次丢手机了。

在 if 条件句中，如果表示与过去的事实相反，要用过去完成时。

　　　　与昨天发生的事实相反，用过去完成时

- If you **had come** earlier yesterday, you would have seen her.

  如果你昨天早点来，你就会见到她了。

Hardly ... when ... 和 No sooner ... than ... 句型中，主句用过去完成时，并且 hardly 和 no sooner 位于句首时引起部分倒装，这两个句型都表示"一……就……"。

- Hardly **had** I **got** home when it stopped raining.

  我一到家，雨就停了。

- **No sooner** had I smelt the flowers **than** I sneezed.

  我一闻见花香，就会打喷嚏。

By the end of + 过去的时间，主语 + had done...

- **By the end of last year**, he **had achieved** the sales target.

  到去年年底，他已经实现了销售目标。

- **By the end of last month**, I **had saved** enough money.

  到上个月底，我已经存了足够多的钱了。

主语 + had done ... + before 从句（从句为一般过去时）

- I **had reached** the station before it began to rain.

  开始下雨前，我就已经到了车站。

- People **had already left** the village before the volcano erupted.

  在火山爆发前，人们就已经离开了这个村庄。

By the time + 从句（从句为一般过去时），主语 + had done ...

- By the time you **invited** us, I **had received** the notice.

  在你邀请我们之前，我已经收到了通知。

- By the time you **arrived**, I **had prepared** everything.

  在你到达之前，我已经准备好了一切。

Exercise

将下面错误的句子改写正确。

1. It was the first time that I lived alone.

_____

2. No sooner the sports meeting started than it began to rain heavily.

_____

3. If it not rained so hard yesterday, we could have gone on a picnic.

_____

4. By the end of last week, they went to many cities.

_____

5. Hardly I got to the bus stop when the bus left.

_____

6. I cleaned the whole house before my mother came back.

_____

7. By the time we reached home, he prepared all the food.

_____

8. I finished my homework before ten o'clock yesterday.

_____

参考答案：

1. It was the first time that I had lived alone.
2. No sooner had the sports meeting started than it began to rain heavily.
3. If it hadn't rained so hard yesterday, we could have gone on a picnic.
4. By the end of last week, they had been to many cities.
5. Hardly had I got to the bus stop when the bus left.
6. I had cleaned the whole house before my mother came back.
7. By the time we reached home, he had prepared all the food.
8. I had finished my homework before ten o'clock yesterday.

第五单元 完成时的疑问句和否定句

现在完成时的疑问句和否定句

1 一般疑问句：把 have/has 提至句首。

- Tom has fixed the car.

  汤姆已经修好了车。　　── 把 has 提到句首

- Has Tom fixed the car yet?

  汤姆已经修好车了吗？

2 特殊疑问句：特殊疑问词 + 一般疑问句的开头 + 其他？

特殊疑问词

- What have you learned from the experience?

  have 提到主语前面，一般疑问句

  你从这次经历中学到了什么？

特殊疑问词

- How many pears have you eaten so far?

  have 提到主语前面，一般疑问句

  到现在为止，你吃了多少个梨？

3 反义疑问句：遵守前肯后否、前否后肯原则。（如果前面的陈述句部分是肯定句，后面的疑问部分要用否定句。反之亦然。）

- Lily has understood what you mean, hasn't she?（前肯后否）

  莉莉已经明白你的意思了，不是吗？

- He hasn't been back, has he?（前否后肯）

  他还没有回来，是吗？

4 否定句：在 have/has 后面 + not。

- Mary has finished her housework.

  玛丽已经完成了她的家务活。── has 后加 not

- Mary hasn't finished her housework.

  玛丽还没有完成她的家务活。

过去完成时的疑问句和否定句

1 一般疑问句：把 had 提至句首。

- He had gone when I got home.

  我到家时他已经走了。　　── 把 had 提到句首

- Had he gone when you got home?

  你回家的时候他已经走了吗？

2 特殊疑问句：特殊疑问词 + 一般疑问句的开头 + 其他？

特殊疑问词

- What had you done before you went to school?　had 提到主语前面，一般疑问句

  你去学校前都做了些什么？

特殊疑问词　　had 提到主语前面，一般疑问句

- Who had he called by the time the police arrived?

  警察到来前，他给谁打电话了？

3 反义疑问句：遵守前肯后否、前否后肯原则。（如果前面的陈述句部分是肯定句，后面的疑问部分要用否定句，反之亦然。）

- She **had come** back before you apologized, **hadn't** she?（前肯后否）
  你还没道歉她就已经回来了，不是吗？
- Lily **hadn't** known what you said before that, **had** she?（前否后肯）
  莉莉不知道你之前说了什么，对吗？

4 否定句：在 had 后面 + not。

had 后加 not

- Katherine had worked for a week till then.
  凯瑟琳那个时候已经工作了一个星期。
- Katherine hadn't worked for a week till then.
  凯瑟琳已经一星期没去工作了。

Exercise

根据要求改写句子。

1. I have seen this dog.（改为否定句）

_____

2. I had prepared all the documents before the manager came in.（改为否定句）

_____

3. Maria has ever been to Thailand.（改为一般疑问句）

_____

4. He had picked up his son before the school was over.（改为一般疑问句）

_____

参考答案：

1. I haven't seen this dog.
2. I hadn't prepared all the documents before the manager came in.
3. Has Maria ever been to Thailand?
4. Had he picked up his son before the school was over?

第十六章

被动语态
Passive Voice

第一单元 被动语态的构成

被动语态用于各种时态中

⊙ 一般现在时的被动语态：am/is/are done

· The classroom **is cleaned** every day.

教室每天都有人打扫。

⊙ 一般过去时的被动语态：was/were done

· My dog **was knocked** down by a car yesterday.

我的狗昨天被一辆车撞倒了。

⊙ 一般将来时的被动语态：shall/will be done

· The meeting **will be held** in our company next week.

会议将于下周在我们公司举行。

⊙ 现在进行时的被动语态：am/is/are being done

· The bridge **is being built** now.

这座桥现在正在建造中。

⊙ 过去进行时的被动语态：was/were being done

· The reading room **was being decorated** when I got there.

当我到那儿时，阅览室正在装修。

⊙ 现在完成时的被动语态：has/have been done

· My key **has been lost** and I can't go home.

我的钥匙丢了，我不能回家了。

⊙ 过去完成时的被动语态：had been done

· The kitchen **had been cleaned** when I got home.

当我到家时，厨房已经打扫过了。

⊙ 过去将来时的被动语态：would be done

· Tony said that the bonus **would be given** to the employees.

托尼说，奖金将发给员工。

⊙ 含有情态动词的被动语态：情态动词 + be done

· The flowers **should be watered** every day.

这些花应该每天浇水。

被动语态的标志是"（情态动词 +）be 动词 + 及物动词的过去分词形式"，其中 be 动词在句子中的形式、数量必须和主语保持一致。

被动语态的运用

1 被动语态强调动作的承受者，主动语态强调动作的执行者。

　　　　强调动作的执行者"Tom"

· Tom **saved** the little dog.

汤姆救了这只小狗。

　　　　　强调动作的承受者"小狗"

· The little dog was **saved** by Tom.

小狗是汤姆救的。

2 被动语态可用于不知道动作的执行者或没必要说明动作的执行者时。

- The hospital **was built** in 2005.
  这家医院建于 2005 年。
- My phone **was stolen** when I was shopping.
  我购物的时候手机被偷了。

3 需要强调动作的对象时，要用被动语态。

- Many trees **were burned** down in the fire.
  许多树在大火中被烧没了。
- The phone **can't be used** in any exams.
  手机不能用在任何考试中。

Exercise

一、从下面四个选项中选出最佳答案。

1. She _____ by that big company.
   A. was employed   B. employed   C. employing   D. employ

2. The air conditioner _____ on.
   A. was turned   B. turned   C. turning   D. turn

3. The cake _____ in the oven now.
   A. was cooked   B. cooked   C. cooking   D. is being cooked

4. The house _____ by these workers.
   A. painting   B. painted   C. was painted   D. paint

5. My computer must _____ by a thief.
   A. stealing   B. have been stolen   C. stolen   D. steal

二、请从下面方框中选择合适的单词，用其正确的形式补全句子。

hold
interview
speak
elect
spend

1. All the money _____ by his son last month.

2. He _____ manager last year.

3. The wedding _____ in the hotel next Monday.

4. Chinese _____ by a lot of people in the world.

5. The businessman _____ by the reporter now.

参考答案：
一、1. A   2. A   3. D   4. C   5. B
二、1. was spent   2. was elected   3. will be held   4. is spoken   5. is being interviewed

第二单元 主动形式表达被动意义

主动形式表示被动

1 **drive，sell，cut，wash，clean，remain** 等词可以表示被动含义。

> 票应该是"被卖"的，但这里的 sell 用主动语态表示被动含义

- The tickets for the play **sell** not well.

这出戏的票卖得不好。

> 刀应该是"被用来切"的，但这里的 cut 用主动语态表示被动含义

- This knife **cuts** sharply.

这把刀很锋利。

2 **taste，smell，look** 等感官动词可以表示被动含义。

> 花应该是"被闻"的，但这里的 smell 用了主动语态表示被动含义

- The flowers **smell** very good.

这些花很好闻。

> 歌应该是"被听"的，但这里的 sound 用了主动语态表示被动含义

- What you sing **sounds** very good.

你唱得很好听。

> 主动语态中，感官动词或 make，let 等使役动词后边跟的是省略 to 的动词不定式，但变为被动语态时，必须加上 to。
> The manager **made Judy do** much work.
> = Judy **was made to** do much work by the manager.
> 经理让朱迪做了很多工作。

3 **need，want，require** 等 词 用 于 **sth need/want/require doing** 结构中时相当于 **sth need/want/require to be done**。

> 电脑应该是"被修理"的，但是这里的 repair 前面有 need 用主动语态表示被动含义

- The computer **needs repairing**.

= The computer **needs to be repaired**.

这台电脑需要修理。

4 **worth doing ...** 结构用主动形式表示被动意义。

> 书应该是"被看"的，但是这里的 read 用于 worth doing ... 结构中，表示被动含义

- His new book is **worth reading**.

他的新书值得一看。

没有被动语态的情况

1 表示"发生、进行"含义的词或词组用主动形式表示被动意义，而且这些词没有被动形式。如 **happen，take place，occur，come true，turn out** 等。

(×) The accident was happened yesterday.

(√) The accident happened yesterday.

事故发生在昨天。

2 系动词没有被动语态

seem	remain
prove	look
smell	taste

(×) The medicine is tasted bitter.

(√) The medicine tastes bitter.
　　　这药吃起来很苦。

3 不及物动词没有被动语态

happen	appear
disappear	rise
emerge	occur

(×) The sun is raised from the east side.

(√) The sun rises from the east side.
　　　太阳从东边升起。

 **Exercise**

一、为下列句子勾选正确的答案。

1. Much work ○ remains ○ is remained to be done.

2. This kind of cake ○ tastes ○ is tasted sweet.

3. His new song is worth ○ listened ○ listening to.

4. My new coat needs ○ ironed ○ ironing.

5. This machine needs to ○ repair ○ be repaired.

二、翻译下面句子。

1. 这件事需要讨论一下。 _____

2. 她的新观点值得采纳。 _____

3. 这种杂志很畅销。 _____

4. 这些货物重 20 吨。 _____

5. 我们都知道冰摸起来是冷的。 _____

参考答案：

一、 1. remains　 2. tastes　 3. listening　 4. ironing　 5. be repaired

二、 1. The matter needs discussing/to be discussed.

　　 2. Her new idea is worth adopting.

　　 3. This kind of magazine sells well.

　　 4. These goods weigh twenty tons.

　　 5. We all know that ice feels cold.

第三单元 主动语态变被动语态

1 主动语态变被动语态，把主动句中的宾语变为主语（如果是代词，要变为主格形式），再把主语变为宾语。

- **They** bought many vegetables. 他们买了很多蔬菜。

- Many vegetables were bought by **them**. 很多蔬菜被他们买了。

2 句子中的谓语动词是短语时，变成被动语态时，不能省略介词。

- My father **turned off** the TV. 我父亲关掉了电视。

- The TV **was turned off** by my father. 电视被我父亲关掉了。

3 主动句的谓语动词若是"情态动词 + 动词原形"，变为被动语态时，将谓语动词变成"情态动词 + be 动词 + 及物动词的过去分词形式"，后面加 **by**。

- We can repair the air conditioner in two days. 我们可以在两天内修好空调。

- The air conditioner can be repaired **by** us in two days. 空调可以在两天内被我们修好。

4 句子中有双宾语时，可以把直接宾语变成主语，在间接宾语前加上恰当的介词。也可以把间接宾语变成主语，直接宾语不变。

- Emma gave me a watch.

  直接宾语 a watch 变成主语

- A watch was given to me by Emma.

  艾玛给了我一块表。 间接宾语 me 前加上介词

- Emma gave me a watch.

  间接宾语 me 变成主语

- I was given a watch by Emma.

  艾玛给了我一块表。 直接宾语 a watch 不变

5 祈使句的主动语态变被动语态，形式为 **Let + 宾语 + be done**。否定形式在 **Let** 后加上 **not** 即可。

Park the car in the parking lot.

把车停在停车场。

Let the car **be parked** in the parking lot.

把车停在停车场。

Don't close the door.

不要关上门。

Let not the door

be closed.

不要关上门。

将下面句子由主动语态变成被动语态，有两种变法的都写出来。

1. Lu Xun wrote this famous novel.

_____

2. Teachers often look after the students.

_____

3. You must turn off the light before you go out.

_____

4. He bought me a dictionary.

_____

_____

5. Our school has built a new library.

_____

6. Mr. Ward teaches us math.

_____

_____

7. Students learn English all over the world.

_____

8. We saw her leave the classroom.

_____

参考答案：

1. This famous novel was written by Lu Xun.

2. The students are often looked after by teachers.

3. The light must be turned off before you go out.

4. I was bought a dictionary by him.   A dictionary was bought for me by him.

5. A new library has been built in our school.

6. Math is taught to us by Mr. Ward.   We are taught math by Mr. Ward.

7. English is learned by students all over the world.

8. She was seen to leave the classroom by us.

第四单元 被动语态和系表结构的区别

1 被动语态结构中的过去分词是动词，是对动作行为进行强调。

动词，对动作行为进行强调
- The shop is **closed** at nine o'clock.

  这个商店九点关门。

系表结构中的过去分词相当于形容词，是对一种状态进行强调。

相当于形容词，对状态进行强调
- The supermarket is **closed** today.

  超市今天没开门。

2 被动语态结构通常可以用介词 **by** 引出动作的执行者。

by 引出动作的执行者 my little son
- The plate was broken **by** my little son.

  盘子被我的小儿子打碎了。

系表结构通常不与介词 **by** 连用

系表结构与 in 连用
- The audience are very **interested** in this feast.

  观众们对这场盛宴非常感兴趣。

3 被动语态通常可以与时间状语、方式状语、地点状语等连用，用 **much**，**greatly** 等可以用来修饰动词的副词来修饰。
- This entertainment program is usually broadcast **in the evening**.

  这个娱乐节目通常是在晚上播出。
- The young man was **greatly** encouraged by his father.

  这个年轻人深受他父亲的鼓励。

系表结构则不可以与状语连用，而通常用副词 **very**，**well**，**quite** 等修饰。
- She is **quite** worried about the final exams.

  她很担心期末考试。
- The bakery is **obviously** closed today.

  这家面包店很显然今天关门了。

4 被动语态可以用于进行时态。

被动语态用于现在进行时
- The new product **is being made**.

  新产品正在生产中。

被动语态用于一般将来时
- The book **will be made** into a film.

  这本书将被拍成电影。

系表结构常用于一般时或者是完成时。

系表结构用于一般现在时
- This bucket **is broken**.

  这个桶是破的。

系表结构用于现在完成时
- We **have been** good friends for many years.

  我们是多年的好朋友了。

Exercise

结合图片，从下面方框中选择合适的动词，用其正确形式填空。

surprise blow surround clean build wash catch do write

1. A new building is _____ around our house now.

2. I am _____ at hearing the news.

3. The house is _____ by the grass.

4. The novel was _____ with great care.

5. The fish is _____ by the fisherman.

6. The trees were _____ away by the flood.

7. The curtain is _____ by the wind.

8. Your room hasn't been _____ yet.

9. The job can only be _____ by her.

参考答案：

1. being built   2. surprised   3. surrounded   4. written   5. caught   6. washed

7. blown   8. cleaned   9. done

223

第十七章

名词性从句
Substantive Clause

第一单元 主语从句

主语从句的引导词
从属连词：that, whether
连接代词：what, whatever,
　　　　　whichever, whoever
连接副词：how, when, where,
　　　　　why

1 从属连词引导的主语从句，可以用 **it** 充当形式主语。**that** 引导的主语从句常位于句首，而且 **that** 不能省略。在含有主语从句的复合句中，谓语动词用单数形式。

• That he can't attend the ceremony is a pity.

= It is a pity that he can't attend the ceremony.

他不能参加这次典礼，真遗憾。

• Whether the problem has been solved is unknown.

这个问题是否已经解决尚不清楚。

that 引导的主语从句用 it 作形式主语的用法已经形成了很多固定用法，主要包含以下几种类型：

a. It + be 动词 + 名词 + that 引导的主语从句

b. It + be 动词 + 形容词 + that 引导的主语从句

c. It + 不及物动词 + that 引导的主语从句

d. It + be 动词 + 过去分词 + that 引导的主语从句

2 连接代词 **what** 引导的主语从句通常位于句首，也可后置，用 **it** 充当形式主语。

• What you said doesn't matter.

你所说的不重要。

• We can't believe what he told us.

我们不能相信他告诉我们的。

• It's not the truth what he told you.

他告诉你的并非实情。

3 连接代词 whatever，whoever，whichever 引导主语从句

• Whatever you want can be earned by yourself.

无论你想要什么，你都可以自己挣来。

• Whoever will be the manager is not important.

无论谁当经理都不重要。

• Whichever projects she accomplished was not perfect.

她完成的任何一个项目都不完美。

4 连接副词引导的主语从句。

• How they are going to leave has not been decided.

他们还没决定如何离开。

• When I will come back depends on the situation.

我什么时候回来要视情况而定。

一、用合适的引导词填空，使句子意思完整。

1. _____ he refused the offer wasn't quite clear.

2. _____ comes to the party will get a bunch of flowers.

3. It's reported _____ four people were injured in the car accident.

4. _____ the sun rises in the east is a well-known fact.

5. _____ matters most in learning knowledge is practice.

二、将下面错误的句子改写正确。

1. Why we will go shopping tomorrow depends on the weather.

_____

2. When the meeting will be held remain a question.

_____

3. That the teacher said is of great importance.

_____

4. Whoever will pick up little Tony has been decided.

_____

5. Whether you do can't make up your mistakes.

_____

参考答案：

一、1. Why   2. Whoever   3. that   4. That   5. What

二、1. Whether we will go shopping tomorrow depends on the weather.

　　2. When the meeting will be held remains a question.

　　3. What the teacher said is of great importance.

　　4. Who will pick up little Tony has been decided.

　　5. Whatever you do can't make up your mistakes.

第二单元 宾语从句1：一般用法

宾语从句的引导词
从属连词：**that, whether, if**
连接代词：**what, which, who,
whom, whose**
连接副词：**how, when, where,
why**

1 从属连词引导的宾语从句，**that** 引导宾语从句时可省略，**whether** 和 **if** 引导宾语从句时不能省略。

· I don't know **(that)** she drops out of school.

我不知道她辍学了。

· I'm not sure **if/whether** I could pass the exam.

我不确定我是否能通过考试。

2 连接代词引导的宾语从句。

· I want to know **who** will win the game.

我想知道谁将赢得这场比赛。

· Can you make out **what** he said?

你能听懂他说的话吗？

3 连接副词引导的宾语从句。

· He asked me **how** I could do it so fast.

他问我怎么能做得这么快。

· I haven't decided **when** I will start my trip.

我还没有决定什么时候开始我的旅行。

whether 和 **if** 的区别：

1. 宾语从句位于句首时，只能用 whether 不能用 if。

（×）If he is handsome or not, I don't care.

（√）**Whether** he is handsome or not, I don't care.

他是否英俊，我不在乎。

2. whether 能和 or not 连用，而 if 不能。

（×）I doubt if it's valuable or not.

（√）I doubt **whether** it's valuable **or not**.

我怀疑它是否有价值。

3. 从句位于介词之后时，只能用 whether 不能用 if。

（×）They are talking about if it will rain tomorrow.

（√）They are talking **about whether** it will rain tomorrow.

他们正在谈论明天是否会下雨。

4. whether 可以接不定式，而 if 不能。

（×）I don't know if to change my job.

（√）I don't know **whether to change** my job.

我不知道是否要换工作。

5. whether 可以引导主语从句和表语从句，而 if 不能。

（×）The problem is if the meeting will be held.

（√）The problem **is whether** the meeting will be held.

问题是会议是否会举行。

Exercise

一、判断下面句子是否为宾语从句。若是，请圈出引导词。

1. I wonder why you can get on well with your colleagues.

2. What he said is not right.

3. Can you tell me who the bag belongs to?

4. I don't know where I can buy some stamps.

5. You can decide whether or not you like something.

二、翻译下面句子。

1. I think that you have made a wrong decision.

_____

2. The manager told us that we must work hard.

_____

3. My mother told me that I shouldn't quarrel with Judy.

_____

4. I think that we should keep quiet in the library.

_____

5. I wonder whether you can deal with the problem all by yourself.

_____

参考答案：

一、1. 是 why 2. 否 3. 是 who 4. 是 where 5. 是 whether

二、1. 我认为你做了一个错误的决定。

　　2. 经理告诉我们，我们必须努力工作。

　　3. 妈妈告诉我，我不应该和朱迪吵架。

　　4. 我认为我们应该在图书馆保持安静。

　　5. 我想知道你是否能独自处理这个难题。

第三单元 宾语从句 2：特殊用法

宾语从句的时态

1 主句是一般现在时，从句可以是任何时态。

> 从句是一般过去时

· I know that he **graduated** last year.

我知道他去年毕业了。

> 从句是一般将来时

· I guess he **is going to** study abroad.

我猜他要出国留学了。

2 主句是过去时，那么从句的时态大多也是过去时（一般过去时、过去进行时、过去将来时、过去完成时）。

> 主句是一般过去时，从句也是一般过去时

· He told me that he **had** an interview with a big company.

他告诉我他去了一家大公司面试。

> 主句的动作和从句的动作同时发生，从句大多用一般过去时或过去进行时

· I heard they **were singing** there.

我听到他们在那里唱歌。

> 从句的动作发生在主句的动作之前，从句用过去完成时

· I was told that he **had passed** the interview.

我被告知他通过了面试。

> 从句的动作发生在主句的动作之后，从句用过去将来时

· He promised that he **would help** the poor.

他承诺他会帮助穷人。

3 当宾语从句说明的是自然现象、客观真理、学科理论、客观事实、谚语或俗语时，无论主句是什么时态，宾语从句都用一般现在时。

> 宾语从句说明的是客观真理，用一般现在时

· We learned that light **travels** faster than sound.

我们早就学过光的传播速度比声音快。

宾语从句的否定转移

主句的主语是第一人称，且其后的谓语动词是 believe（相信），think（认为），expect（期望），suppose（假设）等词时，从句中的否定词要移到主句中。

> 原本强调的是：他不喜欢数学，但英文句子中把否定词放到了主句的主语 I 之后

· I **don't** think he likes math.

我觉得他不喜欢数学。

以下情况中，宾语从句的否定词不能转移到主句中。

1. 主句的主语不是第一人称。

（×）She doesn't think you will come here.

（√）She thinks you won't come here.

　　她认为你不会来。

2. 主句是疑问句。

Can you tell me why you **won't** change your mind?

你能告诉我为什么你不会改变主意吗？

 **Exercise**

一、用括号中所给词的正确时态填空。

1. I don't know what kind of food he _____ (like).

2. I asked Jim how he _____ (go) to school.

3. Everyone knows that it often _____ (rain) in summer.

4. She said she _____ (sleep) at ten yesterday.

5. I hear that he _____ (leave) home a few years ago.

二、用合适的引导词填空，使句子意思完整。

1. We believe _____ she is innocent.

2. I don't know _____ he agreed or not.

3. She suggests_____ we should leave tomorrow.

4. Please tell me _____ one you like best.

5. I have got _____ I wanted.

三、请用合适的关系词合并各题的两个句子。

1. I don't know.   There will be a meeting in ten days.

_____

2. My teacher once told us.   The moon travels around the earth.

_____

3. Tell me.   Are the children playing computer games?

_____

参考答案：

一、1. likes   2. would go   3. rains   4. was sleeping   5. left

二、1. that   2. whether   3. that   4. which   5. what

三、1. I don't know that there will be a meeting in ten days.

  2. My teacher once told us that the moon travels around the earth.

  3. Tell me whether the children are playing computer games.

第四单元 表语从句 1：一般用法

表语从句就是用一个句子作为表语。说明主语是什么或者怎么样，由名词、形容词或相当于名词或形容词的词或短语充当表语。

1 从属连词 that 引导的表语从句。

- The fact is **that** she doesn't work hard.
  事实是她工作不努力。
- The trouble is **that** our company is short of finance.
  问题是我们公司缺乏资金。
- The truth is **that** many cities suffered the flood.
  真相是很多城市都遭受了洪水。

2 从属连词 whether 引导的表语从句。

- The problem is **whether** we will have a holiday.
  问题是我们是否会放假。
- The question is **whether** you can make good use of time.
  问题是你能否好好利用时间。
- The most important thing is **whether** she can finish the project.
  最重要的是她能否完成这个项目。

3 as if，as though 引导表语从句时，这两个词组可位于系动词 be，seem，look，sound，appear 之后。

- It looks **as if** it is going to be windy.
  看来要刮风了。
- It appeared **as though** you were very interested in the topic.
  看起来你对这个话题很感兴趣。

4 连接副词 because，when，where，why，how 引导表语从句。

- It is **because** she always sleeps in class.
  这是因为她经常在课上睡觉。
- The key is **when** you can make progress.
  关键是你何时才能取得进步。
- This is **where** I worked ten years ago.
  这就是我十年前工作的地方。
- This is **why** I don't want to do it.
  这就是为什么我不想这么做的原因。
- This is **how** I come to the top.
  这就是我如何取得成功的。

5 because 引导的表语从句表示原因，why 引导的表语从句表示结果。

表示原因，我迷路了
- It was **because** I got lost on the way home.
  那是因为我在回家的路上迷路了。

表示结果，我不想来这里
- That's **why** I don't want to come here.
  这就是我不想来这里的原因。

Exercise

一、请从框中选出适当的关系词填空。

> why   where   what   whether   because

1. That's _____ we need to do in the morning.

2. I think it is _____ you don't wear heavy coat.

3. This is _____ I once lived.

4. Is that _____ you asked for leave?

5. The question is _____ they will help us.

二、从下面四个选项中选出最佳答案。

1. The reason why she resigned is _____ she was ill.
   A. that   B. when   C. because   D. why

2. The problem is _____ can take the place of the manager.
   A. who   B. whether   C. why   D. how

3. That is _____ we were late for school yesterday.
   A. who   B. when   C. why   D. that

4. You look _____ you were ten years younger.
   A. as   B. as though   C. like   D. why

5. The trouble is _____ we are short of funds.
   A. that   B. how   C. why   D. because

6. The fact is _____ I find this place rather boring.
   A. that   B. when   C. as   D. because

参考答案：
一、1. what   2. because   3. where   4. why   5. whether
二、1. A   2. A   3. C   4. B   5. A   6. A

第五单元 表语从句 2：特殊用法

1 表语从句只能使用陈述语序。

表语从句中使用陈述语序

- The problem is **that** I lost the key.
  问题是我把钥匙丢了。
- The key is **whether** you can find a new job.
  关键是你是否能找到一份新工作。

2 表语从句和主句的时态可以不一致。

- The question **is** who **broke** rules firstly.
  问题是谁先打破了规则。
- She **is** not who I **thought** she was.
  她已经不是我过去想象中的那个人了。

3 That is why 中 why 引导的是表语从句，而 That is the reason why 中 why 引导的是定语从句。

why 引导表语从句

- **That is why** bears hibernate.
  这就是熊冬眠的原因。

why 引导定语从句

- **That is the reason why** you lost your job.
  这就是你失业的原因。

4 如果 what 引导的主语从句，或名词 reason 作主语，后接表语从句来说明某个原因或理由，不用 because，要用 that 引导。

- (×) What made me so sad was because I failed the exam.
- (√) What made me so sad was **that** I failed the exam.
  我这么难过是因为我没有通过考试。
- (×) The reason why she cried was because she lost her computer.
- (√) The reason why she cried was **that** she lost her computer.
  她哭的原因是她丢了电脑。

5 表示建议、劝告、命令的词，如 plan，suggestion，order，proposal，advice 等通常与表语从句连用，此时表语从句的谓语动词要用"should + 动词原形"，其中 should 可以省略。

- My suggestion is that she (should) turn to her parents for help.
  我的建议是她应该向父母寻求帮助。
- The order is that we (should) hand in our paper before next week.
  命令是我们必须在下周前交论文。

Exercise

一、将下面错误的句子改写正确。

1. It sounds as someone is knocking at the door. _____

2. My question is that skipped classes yesterday. _____

3. What I wonder is when did he leave. _____

4. My proposal is that he drives us there. _____

5. The question is what you do it on your own. _____

二、从下面四个选项中选出最佳答案。

1. The truth is _____ the restaurant's turnover is declining.

    A. that   B. when   C. why   D. where

2. The question is _____ the novel is worth reading.

    A. what   B. who   C. where   D. whether

3. It seemed _____ he'd been gone forever.

    A. that   B. as if   C. why   D. where

4. This is the reason _____ I don't agree to the plan.

    A. that   B. who   C. why   D. whether

5. This is _____ I first met you.

    A. that   B. whether   C. /   D. where

参考答案：

一、1. It sounds as if someone is knocking at the door.

    2. My question is who skipped classes yesterday.

    3. What I wonder is when he left.

    4. My proposal is that he (should) drive us there.

    5. The question is how you do it on your own.

二、1. A   2. D   3. B   4. C   5. D

第六单元 同位语从句

同位语从句修饰的名词

answer	belief	conclusion
idea	information	news
promise	suggestion	thought
problem	wish	word
fact	hope	order

- I got **news that** the sports meeting would be put off.

  我得到了运动会将被推迟的消息。

- I have no **idea when** I can decide things on my own.

  我不知道什么时候自己可以决定事情。

同位语从句的引导词

1 that 引导同位语从句的时候，不在句子中担当任何成分，也没有任何实际意义，但是不能省略。

- It's my hope **that** the flight won't be late tomorrow.

  我希望明天的航班不会晚点。

- She made a promise to me **that** she would study hard.

  她向我保证她会努力学习。

- He told me his dream **that** he wanted to be an actor in the future.

  他告诉我他的梦想是长大后想成为一名演员。

2 whether 引导的同位语从句。

- The manager is considering the question **whether** she should be fired.

  经理正在考虑是否要解雇她。

- They discussed the problem **whether** they should go for the project.

  他们讨论了是否应该参加这个项目的问题。

3 如果同位语从句表达的不是完整的意义，那么可以用连接副词和连接代词 how，when，which，where，what，who，why 等来引导。

- I don't know the time **when** I should tell him the truth.

  我不知道应该什么时候告诉他真相。

- I have no idea **why** the meeting was put off.

  我不知道会议为什么被推迟了。

4 表示建议、劝告、命令的词可以和同位语从句连用，此时同位语从句中的谓语动词要用"should + 动词原形"，其中 should 可以省略。

- He gave me advice that I **(should) think** about this thing in a different way.

  他建议我用不同的方式考虑这件事。

- The teacher gave me the suggestion that I **(should) ask** others for help.

  老师建议我，我应该向别人寻求帮助。

Exercise

一、请用合适的连接词合并各题的两个句子。

1. We heard the news.　　Our team had lost. _____

2. I've got the conclusion.　　It's not right to do that. _____

3. This is the fact.　　The money is missing. _____

4. The news is true.　　I will get a pay raise. _____

5. There is some doubt.　　She will come back. _____

二、将下列单词按照正确的顺序排序。

1. suggestion is approved that the meeting be delayed his

_____

2. whether genuine asked me the question the antique he is

_____

3. my wish that want a university I to get into good this is

_____

4. no I have idea when will the start party

_____

参考答案：
一、 1. We heard the news that our team had lost.

　　 2. I've got the conclusion that it's not right to do that.

　　 3. This is the fact that the money is missing.

　　 4. The news that I will get a pay raise is true.

　　 5. There is some doubt whether she will come back.

二、 1. His suggestion that the meeting be delayed is approved.

　　 2. He asked me the question whether the antique is genuine.

　　 3. This is my wish that I want to get into a good university.

　　 4. I have no idea when the party will start.

第十八章

定语从句
Attributive Clause

第一单元 关系词的用法

关系代词的用法

关系代词	所修饰的先行词	在从句中作的成分
who	指人	主语、宾语
whom	指人	宾语
which	指物	主语、宾语
that	指人或物	主语、宾语、表语
whose	指人或物	定语

指人，作主语
- I don't know the woman **that/who** wears a black dress.
  我不认识那个穿黑色连衣裙的女人。

指人，作宾语
- He is the boy **(who/whom/that)** I'm looking for.
  他就是我正寻找的男孩。

指物，作主语
- The building **which/that** stands on the right is a library.
  位于右边的大楼是一座图书馆。

指人，作定语
- There are many people **whose** living conditions are improved now.
  现在许多人的生活条件得到提升。

关系副词的用法

1 where

在从句中作地点状语，可用 in which, on which, at which, to which 等代替。
- This is the hotel **where** I stayed yesterday.
  这就是我昨天住的旅馆。
- This is the house **where**/**in which** my grandparents once lived.
  这是我爷爷奶奶曾经住过的房子。

2 when

在从句中作时间状语，可用 on which, in which, at which, during which 等代替。
- I still remember the day **when** I first came to Japan.
  我还记得我第一次来日本的那一天。
- Valentine's Day is the day **when**/**on which** people express love.
  情人节是人们表达爱的日子。

3 why

在从句中作原因状语，可用 for which 等代替。
- That is the reason **why** I quit the job.
  那就是我辞职的原因。
- I don't know the reason **why**/**for which** he refused to go to your party.
  我不知道他为什么拒绝参加你的聚会。

一、请从下面方框中选择合适的关系代词，可重复选择。

who   that   whom   which   whose

1. Cathy is the student _____ I met yesterday.

2. I like the girl _____ wears white dress.

3. I went to the shopping mall _____ opened yesterday.

4. I know a man _____ father owns a big company.

5. The vase _____ I broke is not expensive.

6. The boy _____ has big eyes is my little brother.

7. The rich lady _____ you talked about is her.

8. This is the lipstick _____ she bought in the mall.

9. I don't know the boy _____ greeted me.

10. David bought a cat _____ leg was injured.

二、选择合适的关系副词填在空格处。

1. The place _____ we played yesterday was too noisy.

2. I will never forget the day _____ we got married.

3. Is it the reason _____ Judy wants to drop out?

4. This is the bakery _____ I always buy bread.

5. Her mother died the year _____ she was born.

6. No one would forget that day _____ the flood hit the city.

7. We met in the park _____ there is a river.

8. We all knew the reason _____ he looked upset.

参考答案：
一、1. that/who/whom   2. that/who   3. that/which   4. whose   5. that/which
      6. that/who   7. that/who/whom   8. that/which   9. that/who   10. whose
二、1. where   2. when   3. why   4. where   5. when   6. when   7. where   8. why

241

第二单元 关系词只用 that 不用 which 的情况

先行词是不定代词，如 anything，nothing，something，everything 等。

- There is **nothing that** I can do for you.
  我不能为你做任何事。
- I can search for **something that** I need on the Internet.
  我可以在互联网上搜索我需要的东西。

先行词被 little，few，much，every，any，all，some，no，each 等词修饰时，只能用 that 引导限制性定语从句。但如果这些词用来修饰人，也可以用 who 引导。
There are few people **who** are in the queue.
排队的人很少。

先行词既有人又有物

- **The writer and his novels that** you like were famous.
  你喜欢的那位作家和他的小说都很有名。
- **The people and things that** he saw in the school left a deep impression on him.
  学校里见到的人和事给他留下了深刻的印象。

先行词被序数词或形容词的最高级修饰

- **The first** mobile phone **that** I bought was broken.
  我买的第一个手机已经坏了。
- This is **the most** terrible food **that** I have ever eaten.
  这是我吃过的最糟糕的食物。

修饰先行词的关系代词在从句中充当表语

- She is no longer the same person **that** she used to **be**.
  她不再是过去的那个她了。
- He is not the rich person **that** he used to **be** ten years ago.
  他不再是十年前那个富有的人了。

先行词被 the very，the same，the only，the last 等修饰

- It's **the very** wallet **that** I'm looking for.
  这正是我在寻找的钱包。
- She is **the only** girl **that** won the race.
  她是唯一赢得比赛的女孩。

主句是 which，who 等疑问代词引导的疑问句

- **Which** route is the best **that** we should take?
  我们要走哪条路线最好？
- **Who** is the man **that** helps you?
  谁是帮助你的人？

 **Exercise**

一、请用 that 或 which 填空，完成句子。

1. Tina didn't tell her mother all _____ had happened.

2. Which is the fruit _____ you like best?

3. The meeting _____ you missed is very important.

4. I dislike the cake _____ you bought yesterday.

5. This is the only clue _____ I could find.

6. This is the very porcelain _____ my father wants to buy.

7. It is the most delicious cake _____ I have had.

8. This is the book _____ I am looking for.

9. The woman and her pet _____ are walking towards us attract great attention.

10. The station _____ was newly built is forty miles far away my house.

二、为下列句子勾选正确的答案。

1. He is the kind person ○ who ○ which helped me.

2. The lady ○ who ○ whose two daughters are both doctors was in hospital.

3. Do you see the woman ○ who ○ whose was on the bus?

4. This is the most enjoyable show ○ that ○ which I have ever seen.

5. He is the last person ○ that ○ which I want to see.

6. I intend to visit the town ○ that ○ where there is beautiful scenery.

7. The room ○ that ○ whose window faces north is mine.

8. You should write down everything ○ that ○ which you think is important.

参考答案：
一、1. that   2. that   3. that/which   4. that/which   5. that
    6. that   7. that   8. that/which   9. that   10. that/which
二、1. who   2. whose   3. who   4. that   5. that   6. where   7. whose   8. that

第三单元 限制性定语从句与非限制性定语从句的区别

形式不同

限制性定语从句不用逗号和主句隔开。	非限制性定语从句用逗号和主句隔开。
· You are the only person **that is willing to help me**. 你是唯一一个愿意帮助我的人。	· Beijing, **which is the capital of China**, has many places of interest. 北京是中国的首都，它有许多名胜古迹。
· The man **who wears a black hat** is very handsome. 戴黑帽子的那个人很英俊。	· The computer, **which was bought last year**, was out of date. 去年买的那台电脑已经过时了。

意义不同

限制性定语从句不可省略，对先行词起限定作用。

不可省略，对 patient 起限定作用

· He is the patient **that/whom I am looking after**.

他就是我正在照顾的病人。

不可省略，对 building 起限定作用

· It is the tallest building **that I have ever seen**.

这是我见过的最高的建筑物。

非限制性定语从句可以省略，只是对先行词进行补充说明。

· I bought a coat for my mother as a present, **which made her happy.**

可以省略，对 present 补充说明

我给妈妈买了一件外套作为礼物，这让她很高兴。

可以省略，对 woman 补充说明

· The woman, **whose son is a doctor**, has retired.

这个女人已经退休了，她的儿子是一名医生。

关系词用法不同

限制性定语从句关系词作宾语时可省略；能用 **that**；能用 **who** 代替 **whom**。

· This is the boy **(that)** he worked with in the hospital.

· This is the boy **who/whom** he worked with in the hospital.

这就是那个在医院和他一起工作的男孩。

非限制性定语从句关系词不可省略；不能用 **that**；不能用 **who** 代替 **whom**。

(×) The woman, that/who you met in my room, was a tutor.

(√) The woman, **whom you met in my room**, was a tutor.

你在我房间里见过的那个女人是个家庭教师。

一、请判断下面句子是"限制性定语从句"还是"非限制性定语从句"。请在"限制性定语从句"前写上"R", "非限制性定语从句"前写上"N"。

_____ 1. He didn't do it in the way I told him.

_____ 2. The earth moves round the sun, which is known to us.

_____ 3. Cathy, who is our teacher, just graduated last year.

_____ 4. This is the gentleman I met on the street.

_____ 5. She has finished the task, which was easy for her.

_____ 6. We traveled to Xi'an, where there are all kinds of delicious food.

_____ 7. She is the woman whose car was broken.

_____ 8. My son, who is in Japan, is coming home next week.

_____ 9. I invite Jim, who is my best friend.

_____ 10. People who take physical exercise are healthier.

二、用合适的引导词填空，使句子意思完整。

1. The present is from my sister, _____ is working in Shanghai.

2. You are the only person _____ I can trust.

3. I lost a book _____ name I can't remember.

4. Smoking, _____ is a bad habit, is popular among men.

5. This is the bike _____ my mother bought me for my birthday.

参考答案：

一、1. R　2. N　3. N　4. R　5. N　6. N　7. R　8. N　9. N　10. R

二、1. who　2. that　3. whose　4. which　5. that/which

245

第四单元 关系词 as 和 which 引导的非限制性定语从句

1 as 和 which 在所引导的非限制性定语从句中作主语或宾语，修饰前面的整个句子。as 和 which 可以互换。

• The road is crowded, as/which we can see.

我们能看到这条路很拥挤。

2 先行词被 such, the same 修饰时，一般由 as 而不是 which 来引导非限制性定语从句。

（×）This is the same computer which I bought.

（√）This is the same computer as I bought.

这和我买的电脑一样。

（×）No one is such a fool which you look.

（√）No one is such a fool as you look.

没有人看起来像你一样傻。

1. 先行词被 the same 修饰、且定语从句由 that 引导时，通常表示同一件事物。而由 as 引导时，通常表示不同的事物（只是一类而已）。

It's the same bike that you rode.

这就是你骑过的那辆车。

I have the same bicycle as you bought.

我的自行车和你买的一样。

2. such... as 引导的是定语从句，as 在从句中作主语和宾语，而 such ... that 引导的是结果状语从句，that 在从句中不做成分。

This is such a good novel as I want to read.

This is such a good novel that I want to read it.

这是一本不错的小说，正是我想读的。

3 as 引导的非限制性定语从句的位置比较灵活，可位于句首、句中和句末。而 which 引导的非限制性定语从句只能位于句末。

位于句首

• As we all know, the environment is getting worse and worse.

我们都知道，环境变得越来越糟。

位于句中

• Defoe, as we all know, is a famous litterateur.

正如我们所知道的，笛福是一位著名的文学家。

位于句末

• The city is famous for tea, as we all know.

我们都知道，这个城市以茶而闻名。

• The Great Wall is one of the Seven Wonders of the World, which is known to all.

只能位于句末

众所周知，长城是世界七大奇迹之一。

4 主句和从句存在逻辑上的因果关系时，一般用 which 来引导从句。

• She decided to study abroad, which made her parents happy.

她决定出国留学，这让父母很高兴。

• A lot of people entered the station, which made the hall crowded.

很多人进入车站，这使大厅很拥挤。

Exercise

一、将下面错误的句子改写正确。

1. It is such a wonderful film as I want to see it again.

_____

2. I forgot the keys, as made things worse.

_____

3. Which we know, lemons taste sour.

_____

4. He was wearing the same shoes as he had on yesterday.

_____

二、请用 as 或 which 填空，完成句子。

1. _____ we all know, Taylor Swift is a famous singer.

2. I have the same coat _____ your mother bought for you.

3. He changed his mind, _____ made us relaxed.

4. He never quits smoking, _____ is known to all.

5. This is such a good film _____ I want to see.

6. The party was put off, _____ is not what we wanted.

7. He told us he lost the game, _____ was a lie.

8. _____ is known to all, people can't live without air.

参考答案：

一、1. It is such a wonderful film that I want to see it again./It is such a wonderful film as I want to see again.

2. I forgot the keys, which made things worse.

3. As we know, lemons taste sour.

4. He was wearing the same shoes that he had on yesterday.

二、1. As 2. as 3. which 4. as/which 5. as 6. as/which 7. as/which 8. As

第五单元 定语从句和同位语从句的区别

引导词不同

定语从句由关系代词和关系副词引导。

定语从句由关系代词 whose 引导
- I have a cat **whose** fur is white.

我有一只猫，它的毛是白色的。

定语从句由关系副词 when 引导
- They left yesterday **when** the rain stopped.

他们昨天离开了，那时候雨停了。

同位语从句多由 that 引导，有时也由 when，how，where，why，whether，who，what 等引导。

同位语从句由 that 引导
- I heard the news **that** her father died yesterday.

我昨天听到了她父亲去世的消息。

同位语从句由 when 引导
- I have no idea **when** you can get my letter.

我不知道你什么时候能收到我的信。

引导词在句中所作成分的区别

定语从句的引导词可在从句中作主语、宾语、定语或者状语。that 引导定语从句作宾语时可以省略。

who 在定语从句中作主语
- I make friends with Judy **who** has big eyes.

我和有着大眼睛的朱迪交了朋友。

that 在从句中作宾语，可以省略
- This is a picture **(that)** I bought yesterday.

这是我昨天买的一幅画。

同位语从句的引导词不在句中作任何成分，that 引导同位语从句时虽然不在句中作任何成分，但是不能省略。

that 在从句中不作任何成分
- I heard the news **that** we would have two days off.

我听到一个消息，我们要放两天假。

that 在从句中不可以省略
- I know her thought **that** she wants to be an actress.

我知道她想当演员的想法。

从句与先行词的关系不同

定语从句对先行词起修饰、限定作用。

that you saw 修饰 the man
- The man **that you saw** just now is my boyfriend.

你刚才看到的那个人是我的男朋友。

同位语从句对先行词的内容进行补充说明。

that she will study hard 是对 promise 的补充说明
- Don't believe her promise **that she will study hard**.

别相信她会努力学习的诺言。

先行词不同

定语从句的先行词可以是名词、代词、主句的一部分或完整的句子。

- **The class** that you skipped yesterday was very important.
  你昨天逃的那节课很重要。
- **The girl** who is sweeping the floor is my best friend.
  正在扫地的那个女孩是我最好的朋友。

同位语从句的先行词只能是 promise，conclusion，wish，fact，belief，idea，thought，truth 等抽象名词。

- This is **the fact** that we don't have enough money.
  这就是我们没有足够钱的事实。
- He expressed his **thought** that he wanted to be the monitor.
  他表达了他想当班长的想法。

 Exercise

请判断下面句子是"定语从句"还是"同位语从句"。请在"定语从句"前写上"A"，"同位语从句"前写上"B"。

_____ 1. The apartment I bought is very valuable.

_____ 2. The news that we are having a holiday is true.

_____ 3. I have no idea why she left.

_____ 4. This is the man who started the hotel.

_____ 5. I still remember the day when I first met you.

_____ 6. There is some doubt whether she will come back.

_____ 7. The novels she wrote are very popular.

_____ 8. There is no doubt that she is an honest woman.

_____ 9. The news that she won the lottery shocked us.

_____ 10. This is the photo which I took in Beijing.

参考答案：

1. A   2. B   3. B   4. A   5. A   6. B   7. A   8. B   9. B   10. A

第十九章

状语从句
Adverbial Clause

第一单元 时间状语从句

when

when 表示"当……时候",引导的时间状语从句中的谓语动词可以是延续性或瞬间动词。主句和从句的动作可以同时发生或者先后发生。

· **When** he came to me, I was in the bathroom. (同时发生)

当他来找我的时候,我正在卫生间。

· The boss asked him **when** the project would be completed. (先后发生)

老板问他这个项目什么时候能完成。

while

while 引导时间状语的时候,从句中的谓语动词必须是延续性动词或者表示状态的动词。主句和从句的动作需要同时发生。如果时间状语从句中的谓语动词是延续性动词且主句和从句的动作同时发生,**when** 和 **while** 可以互换。

· While she is doing her homework, her grandfather is playing the guitar in the living room.

她在写作业的时候,他祖父正在客厅弹吉他。

· **While/When** she was shopping, a stranger was following her.

当她在逛街的时候,一个陌生人正尾随着她。

as

as 表示"一边……一边",引导时间状语从句时通常表示两个接连发生的动作或者同时进行的动作。如果时间状语从句的谓语动词是瞬间性动词,且主句和从句的动作同时发生时,**as** 和 **when** 可以互换。

· Tony can sing **as** he plays the guitar.

托尼可以一边唱歌,一边弹吉他。

· **As/When** the assistant sent the boss to the airport, he met his ex-girlfriend.

助理在送老板去机场的时候,遇到了他的前女友。

since

since 表示"自从",引导时间状语从句的时候,主句用现在完成时,从句用一般过去时。如果谓语动词是延续性动词,则表示该动作已经完成;如果谓语动词是瞬间性动词,则表示该动作的开始。

· I haven't seen Charlie and Alice **since** they married. (动作的开始)

自从查理和爱丽丝结婚后,我就再也没有见过他们。

· I haven't got any information about them **since** they lived here. (动作的结束)

自从他们不住在这儿之后,我就没有得知任何关于他们的消息。

until, till

until 和 **till** 在一般情况下可以互换。但是句中如果有否定词的话，多用 **until**。**not ... until ...** 的意思是"直到……才"。此外，**until** 可以用于强调句中。

- Until/Till graduating from college, she kept her elementary school diary.
  直到大学毕业，她还保留着小学的日记。
- I did **not** receive the gift **until** the next day of Christmas.
  直到圣诞节第二天，我才收到礼物。

before, after

1 **before** 的意思是"在……之前"，表示从句的动作发生在主句之前。在引导时间状语从句的时候，如果主句是将来时，从句一般用现在时；如果主句用过去完成时，从句通常用一般过去时。**before** 有的时候还可以理解为"……之后才……"。

- Hurry up, we're going to get to the airport **before** the plane takes off.
  快点，我们要在飞机起飞之前到达机场。
- Before the police arrived, the criminals had destroyed all the evidence.
  在警察到达之前，罪犯已经把所有的证据都毁灭了。

2 **after** 的意思是"在……之后"，表示从句的动作发生在主句之后。

- After the epidemic broke out in this city, it was locked down.
  在疫情爆发之后，这座城市封城了。

by the time

by the time 表示"到……时候"，在引导时间状语从句的时候，如果从句用一般现在时，主句用将来完成时；如果从句用一般过去时，主句则用过去完成时。

- By the time you are ready to take action, I will have completed the experiment.
  到你准备采取措施的时候，我都已经完成实验了。
- By the time I got home, my little daughter had fallen asleep.
  当我回到家中的时候，我的小女儿已经进入梦乡。

each time，next time 等名词短语

- Each time I chat with my father, I learn something from him.
  每次和父亲聊天，我都能从他身上学到些什么。
- She promised to introduce Cindy to me the **next time** we met her.
  她承诺下次见到辛迪的时候，介绍她给我认识。

as soon as, no sooner than, the moment

as soon as，no sooner than，the moment 表示"一……就……"。

- I saw him **as soon as** I got off the plane.
  我一下飞机就看到了他。
- The **minute** I heard the good news, I shared it with my grandma.
  我一得知这个好消息，就和我的奶奶分享它了。

第二单元 地点、方式状语从句

where

where 可引导状语从句，其引导的从句在整个句子充当地点状语。

- Put the key **where** it used to be.

  把钥匙放在原来的地方。

- You'd better wait for him **where** he lives.

  你最好在他住的地方等他。

- The telescope was left **where** I sat just now.

  望远镜被遗忘在我刚才坐过的地方。

wherever, anywhere

wherever 和 **anywhere** 表示"任何地方，无论何处"，引导地点状语从句时，可以置于主句之前，也可以置于主句之后。

- You can go **wherever** you like after you grow up.

  你长大后可以去任何你喜欢的地方。

- You can put your toys in your bedroom **anywhere** you like.

  你可以把玩具随便放在卧室的什么地方都行。

as

as 的意思是"正如……"，引导方式状语从句的时候通常位于主句之后。

- She ended up getting into university just **as** her mom had expected.

  她最终考上了大学，就像她妈妈所期待的那样。

- **As** we can see, he lied to all of us.

  正如我们所看到的，他向所有人撒了谎。

as if, as though

as if 和 **as though** 引导方式状语从句的时候意思是"好像、仿佛"。如果表示与某个事实相反，则用虚拟语气；如果所述情况是事实或实现的可能性较大，则用陈述语气。

- The girl dyed her hair white, **as if** she were an old woman.

  这个女孩将头发染成了白色，好似一位老人。

- She sat motionless on the sofa, **as if** she had fallen asleep.

  她坐在沙发上一动不动，好似睡着了。

一、为下列句子勾选正确的答案。

1. ○ **Where** ○ **Wherever** he goes, there are some crazy fans waiting for him.

2. ○ **Where** ○ **Wherever** there is an accident, you can see the policeman.

3. ○ **After** ○ **Before** I prepared everything well, I left the town.

4. It is a year ○ **since** ○ **for** his girlfriend promised to marry him.

二、从 A 栏和 B 栏中选出语意搭配的从句，并用 where 连接构成一个新的句子。

there is a supermarket   he wants to live   the school was built

it is near to the sea   we can buy various of items   used to be a temple

1. _____

2. _____

3. _____

参考答案：

一、1. Wherever   2. Where   3. After   4. since

二、1. There is a supermarket where we can buy various of items.

　　2. The school was built where there used to be a temple.

　　3. He wants to live where it is near to the sea.

第三单元 原因状语从句

because

because 表示已知或未知的事实，表示原因时语气最强，常用来回答 **why** 的提问。通常位于主句之后。

- Bob was fired by the company because he leaked confidential documents from the company.

  鲍勃被公司辞退了，因为他泄露了公司的机密文件。

- My aunt likes going shopping in Hong Kong because the goods there are cheaper.

  我姑姑喜欢去香港购物，因为那里的商品更便宜。

because 用来说明人们不知道的原因，而 as 和 since 用来说明众人都知道的原因。because 引导的原因状语从句位于句末，用逗号和主句隔开，这种情况下 for 可以代替 because。

for

for 在引导原因状语从句的时候，有的情况下可以和 **because** 互换。但是如果表示对某种情况的推测，而不是真实原因的时候，只能用 **for**。

- I'm sleepy now, for/because I stayed up all night to write plans last night.

  我现在很困，因为我昨天晚上熬通宵写方案。

- She must be hungry, for she ate nothing today.

  她肯定饿了，因为她今天什么东西也没吃。

now that

now that 的意思是"既然"，因果关系比较弱，通常用于口语中。

- Now that you know everything, there's no need for me to hide it.

  既然你已经知道所有的事情，那我也没有必要隐瞒了。

- Now that we're divorced, I'll move out of the house as soon as possible.

  既然我们已经离婚了，我会尽快从房子里搬出去。

as

as 语气较弱，通常指的是显而易见的原因，常位于主句之前。

- **As** she had done similar work before, she ran the program with a light touch.
  因为之前做过类似的工作，这个项目她做起来得心应手。
- **As** our parents are friends, we knew each other from an early age.
  因为我们的父母是朋友，我们从小就认识。

since

since 的意思是"既然"，通常指的是对方已知的事实，常位于主句之前。

- **Since** you're not going home for Christmas, you'd better return the ticket.
  既然你不打算回家过圣诞节，那你最好把机票退了吧。
- **Since** you made a promise, you should try to deliver on it.
  既然你做出承诺，那就应该努力兑现。

 **Exercise**

一、为下列句子勾选正确的答案。

1. ○ **Since** ○ **As** we grow up together, I understand his character totally.

2. She failed the exam ○ **because of** ○ **because** her carelessness.

3. The boy seems very upset, ○ **for** ○ **since** he didn't pass the final examination.

4. George gives up the job ○ **since** ○ **because of** the low salary.

5. ○ **Now that** ○ **So** you don't want to know anything about him, I will say nothing from now on.

二、找出下列句子的错误之处并改正。

1. They quarreled as they couldn't reach a common view on their children's education. _____

2. They saved on food and expenses since he made investments in stock market with all savings. _____

3. That you have found a job, you should earn your living all by yourself. _____

4. She is in a bad mood, since she broke up with her boyfriend. _____

5. As for we are a team, I trust you totally. _____

参考答案：
一、1. As   2. because of   3. for   4. because of   5. Now that
二、1. as → because   2. saved 前加 have   3. That → Now that
        4. since → for   5. 去掉 for

第四单元 条件状语从句

if

if 引导的条件状语从句中，从句的谓语动词用一般现在时，主句用一般将来时。从句的谓语动词用现在完成时，主句用一般现在时。

- **If** it snows heavily tomorrow, we will work at home.

  如果明天下大雪，我们将在家办公。

- **If** you choose to be a teacher, you will be responsible for the whole class.

  如果你选择成为一名教师，你将要对班上的所有学生负责。

> 需要注意的是，if 引导条件状语从句时，从句不能用将来时和进行时。if 引导的条件状语从句可位于句首也可位于句末。if 引导条件状语从句时，主句还可以用祈使句来表示。
> **If you feel unhappy, tell me.** 如果你感到不开心，告诉我。

only if, if only

only if 的意思是"只有……"，引导的条件状语从句位于句首，且中间没有逗号隔开的时候，主句要倒装。**if only** 的意思是"要是……就好了"，通常用来引导虚拟语气。

- **Only if** you have made an appointment in advance will you meet the chairman.

  只有提前预约过，才能见到董事长。

- **If only** my father were a rich man.

  要是我爸爸是个富豪就好了。

so/as long as

as long as, so long as 引导条件状语从句时表示"只要……"。

- **As long as** you practice every day, your spoken French level will be improved.

  只要你每天练习，你的法语口语水平就会得到提升。

- You will not be punished **so long as** you explain the situation to the supervisor.

  只要你跟主管说明情况，就不会受到处罚。

unless

unless "除非"引导条件状语从句，相当于 **if not**。

- I won't forgive him **unless** he apologizes to me.

  除非他向我道歉，否则我不会原谅他的。

- Many employees will leave **unless** our company provides better benefits for us.

  除非我们公司给员工提供更好的福利，否则很多员工都会离职。

supposed/supposing that

supposed/supposing that 表示"假如"，引导的条件状语从句一般位于主句之前。

- **Supposed that** you don't answer the phone, we'll call the police.

  如果你不接电话的话，我们就报警了。

provided/providing that

provided/providing that 也表示"假如"，用法和 **supposed that** 一样。

- **Providing that** he doesn't come in time, we won't open the door.

  如果他没有及时赶来的话，我们今天就打不开门。

 **Exercise**

从下列四个选项中选出正确答案。

1. _____ he insists to do that, he must pay a heavy price for it.

   A. Unless   B. So   C. If   D. If only

2. _____ I were a bird!

   A. Only if   B. If only   C. So long as   D. As long as

3. _____ you satisfy my demand, I will do as you said.

   A. Since   B. In order   C. As long as   D. Unless

4. _____ you succeeded, you had been very old.

   A. Only if   B. Next time   C. Before   D. By the time

5. She was ill _____ I met her.

   A. the last time   B. for   C. what   D. unless

6. _____ that she doesn't get there on time, you will lose your life.

   A. If   B. Provided   C. So   D. Such

7. She will have nothing at all _____ she leaves her parents.

   A. on condition that   B. when   C. unless   D. while

8. _____ she behaves well in the company can she get a promotion.

   A. What   B. Who   C. Only if   D. If only

参考答案：

1. C   2. B   3. C   4. D   5. A   6. B   7. A   8. C

第五单元 结果状语从句

so ... that ...

so... that... 引导结果状语从句的时候，**so** 用来修饰形容词或副词。

- He is **so** charming **that** the girls in our school all like him.

  他十分有魅力，我们学校里的女孩子都喜欢他。

- Charles slept **so** late yesterday **that** he was late this morning.

  查尔斯昨天睡得太晚，以至于今天早上迟到了。

- The car is **so** small **that** there is no extra place to put a suitcase.

  这辆车太小了，没有多余的地方放行李箱。

so ... that ... 引导的结果状语从句还有另外一种形式，即 "so + many/much/few/little + 名词 + that + 其他"。
There is so few money in the card that I can't afford to buy anything. 卡里几乎没有钱，以至于我付不起钱买任何东西。

such ... that ...

such ... that ... 引导结果状语从句的时候，**such** 用来修饰名词。

- Many foreign friends think that Chinese is **such** a difficult language **that** they can't learn well without teachers.

  许多外国朋友都认为汉语是一门很难学的语言，没有老师的情况下很难学会。

- Mr. Smith came up with **such** a good idea **that** we solved the current problem.

  史密斯先生提出了一个好主意，我们解决了当下的难题。

so, so that

- I lost my mother's necklace **so** I hid in the house and didn't dare to go out.

  我把妈妈的项链弄丢了，因此躲在屋里不敢出去。

- The company Mary worked for went bankrupt **so that** she lost her job.

  玛丽工作的那家公司破产了，于是她就失业了。

一、找出下列句子的错误之处并改正。

1. The alarm clock was broken such that I was late for school. _____

2. The basketball player was so a skillful that he had plenty of fans. _____

3. The meeting was so bored that I fell asleep in the end. _____

4. He puts forward such great idea that we all agree on it. _____

5. The elevator goes wrong so that they had to take the stairs. _____

二、请分别用 so ... that ..., such ... that ... 将下面的句子合成一句话。

1. It is a cute baby.   I want to kiss her face.

_____

_____

2. He is a brave man.   We all respect him.

_____

_____

3. The car is heavy.   No one can hold up with it.

_____

_____

_____

参考答案：

一、1. such → so   2. 去掉 a   3. bored → boring   4. such 后面加 a   5. goes → went

二、1. It is such a cute baby that I want to kiss her face.

     The baby is so cute that I want to kiss her face.

  2. He is such a brave man that we all respect him.

     He is so brave that we all respect him.

  3. It is such a heavy car that no one can hold up with it.

     The car is so heavy that no one can hold up with it.

第六单元 让步状语从句

though, although

though 和 **although** 意为"尽管",在引导让步状语从句的时候,一般情况下是可以互换的,但是 **although** 一般比 **though** 正式一些。**though** 和 **although** 在引导让步状语从句的时候,不能和 **but** 连用,但是可以和 **yet, still** 连用。

- **Although** he has little money, he wants to buy a car.

  尽管几乎没钱,他还是想买一辆车。

- **Though** they live in different cities, they still keep in touch with each other.

  尽管他们生活在不同城市,但他们彼此之间依旧保持联系。

even if, even though

even if 和 **even though** 的意思是"即使",引导让步状语从句时常位于句首。

- **Even if** it was cold outside, she still wore one skirt.

  即使外面很冷,她还是只穿了一条短裙。

- **Even though** he was sick, he was reluctant to take medicine.

  即使他生病了,他还是不愿意吃药。

whether ... (or not ...)

whether ... (or not ...) 的意思是"无论……都"。

- **Whether** it works **or not**, I'll try it.

  无论能否成功,我都会尝试一下。

as, though

as 和 **though** 引导的让步状语从句中的表语和状语部分可以提前。

①句首是名词,则名词前边不需要用冠词。

②句首是实义动词,助动词放于主语之后。

③形容词或副词也可以提前。

- Adult **though/as** he is, he still lives of his parents.

  虽然他是一个成年人了,但他仍在"啃老"。

- Work hard **though/as** they do, the parents still cannot afford their children's school fees.

  虽然他们努力工作,但这对父母仍负担不起子女的学费。

- Wealthy **though/as** he is, he is never willing to help the poor.

  虽然他很富有,但他从来不愿意对穷人施以援手。

"no matter + 疑问词" 或 "疑问词 + ever"

- **No matter what** job you choose to do, you should try your best to do it well.

  无论你选择做什么工作,你都应该尽自己最大努力做好。

- **Whichever** dress you pick, I'll buy it for you.

  无论你挑选哪件衣服,我都会给你买。

一、为下列句子勾选正确的答案。

1. Although they quarreled every day, ○ but ○ / they did not divorce.

2. ○ Even if ○ Whatever Mike apologized, I still couldn't forgive him.

3. Kid ○ although ○ though he is, he can take care of his own affairs.

4. ○ Whether ○ If you pass the interview, you will receive an email from our company.

5. ○ Whatever ○ Whichever you want to do, I'll support you.

二、请使用括号内的提示词将两个句子合并起来。

1. He is unwilling to see me.　He still comes. (even if)

_____

2. She was ill.　She went to work. (though)

_____

3. He was kind to her.　She felt his indifference. (although，yet)

_____

4. He was rich.　He never showed off his wealth. (as)

_____

5. You are honest to me.　I don't believe your words. (whether)

_____

参考答案：

一、1. /　2. Even if　3. though　4. If　5. Whatever

二、1. Even if he is unwilling to see me, he still comes.

　　2. Though she was ill, she went to work.

　　3. Although he was kind to her, yet she felt his indifference.

　　4. Rich as he was, he never showed off his wealth. = As he was rich, he never showed off his wealth.

　　5. Whether you are honest to me or not, I don't believe your words.

第七单元 目的状语从句

so that

so that 引导目的状语从句与结果状语从句的不同之处在于，目的状语从句中经常会出现情态动词。so that 引导的目的状语从句通常位于句尾。

· Please throw garbage in the trash so that the floor can be kept clean.

请将垃圾丢进垃圾桶，以保持地面整洁。

· He runs as fast as he could so that he can catch up with the bus.

他跑得飞快，以便追上公交车。

in order that

in order that 在引导目的状语从句的时候，从句中常会出现情态动词。in order that 引导的目的状语从句既可以位于主句之前也可以位于主语之后。

· In order that he could earn enough money to treat his mother, he broke the law.

为了能赚到足够的钱给母亲治病，他触犯了法律。

· He prepared the party in order that he could give a surprise to his wife.

为了给妻子一个惊喜，他准备了这场聚会。

in case, for fear that, lest

in case, for fear that, lest 在引导目的状语从句的时候，谓语动词通常用虚拟语气，即"should + 动词原形"，其中 should 可以省略；如果不用虚拟语气的话，从句通常用一般现在时或一般过去时。

· You'd better bring an umbrella at the door in case you get wet in the rain.

你最好带上门口的雨伞，以免下雨淋湿。

· We need to keep our voice down for fear that we should wake grandpa up.

我们声音小点儿，以免吵醒爷爷。

· You had better speak less lest she should get angry.

你要少说话以免惹她生气。

比较：

in order to 后跟动词词组，in order that 后接完整的句子。

In order to propose to her, he prepared a candlelit dinner.

In order that he could propose to her, he prepared a candlelit dinner.

为了向她求婚，他准备了烛光晚餐。

Exercise

一、从下面四个选项中选出最佳答案。

1. We must get there earlier _____ we can buy Bing Dwen Dwen.

   A. such that   B. so that   C. in order to   D. in order

2. Alice speaks loudly _____ she can quiet the students in the classroom.

   A. so that   B. in order to   C. since   D. because

3. _____ the clown could see them, they waved to the stage.

   A. So that   B. For   C. In order that   D. If

4. Factories must produce a lot of masks _____ meet the needs of everyone's epidemic prevention.

   A. in order that   B. such that   C. so that   D. in order to

5. _____ they can provide better living conditions for their children, the couple went to the city to work.

   A. Unless   B. In order that   C. In case   D. As soon as

二、找出下列句子的错误之处并改正。

1. You need to consider it carefully in case that you regret. _____

2. You'd better tell him the truth for fear he should be worried about you. _____

3. Be careful lest you should burnt by the fire. _____

4. He opened the window such that the smoke could get out of the house. _____

5. The math teacher has spoken many times in order to we can understand. _____

参考答案:

一、1. B   2. A   3. C   4. D   5. B

二、1. 去掉 that   2. fear 后加 that   3. should 后加 be

　　4. such → so   5. to → that

第二十章

特殊句式
Special
Sentence Patterns

第一单元 插入语

插入语是对一句话作附加说明，将它删除后，句子结构仍然完整。

1 形容词（短语）作插入语。

true	wonderful
excellent	strange to say
most important of all	
sure enough	

- **True**, the show is so wonderful.
  真的，表演太精彩了。
- **Strange to say**, the manager hasn't come to work for several days.
  说来奇怪，经理好几天没来上班了。

2 副词（短语）作插入语。

indeed	surely	frankly
certainly	however	generally
personally	honestly	fortunately
luckily	though	besides
exactly	probably	or rather
otherwise	perhaps	maybe

- **However**, he overestimated his own abilities.
  然而，他高估了自己的能力。
- Keep the window closed, **otherwise** you'll catch a cold.
  把窗户关好，否则你会感冒的。

3 介词短语作插入语。

in fact	in one's opinion
in general	in a word
on the contrary	to one's surprise
in other words	in a few words
of course	by the way
as a result	for example
in brief	in short
on the other hand	in conclusion

- **In fact**, it is difficult for me to do the experiment.
  事实上，做这项实验对我来说很困难。
- **By the way**, I'm going to the milk tea shop.
  顺便说一下，我要去奶茶店。

4 V-ing（短语）作插入语。

talking of
considering
judging from/by
generally speaking
strictly speaking

Generally speaking, the weather there is so cold.
一般来说，那里的天气很冷。
Strictly speaking, what you just said is not right.
严格来说，你所说的是不正确的。

5 不定式短语作插入语。

to be frank	to be honest
to be sure	to sum up
to start with	to begin with
to tell you the truth	
to make matters worse	

- **To sum up**, this problem is easy to solve.
  总之，这个问题很容易解决。
- **To be honest**, the house is too expensive for us.
  老实说，这房子的价格对我们来说太贵了。

6 句子（陈述句和一般疑问句）作插入语。

I suppose	I hope	I'm afraid
you see	I am sure	I believe
I think	I know	as I see
what's more		as we know

- **What's more**, you should set a good example to your children.
  更重要的是，你应该为你的孩子树立一个好的榜样。
- **As we all know**, the scenery of the West Lake is very beautiful.
  我们都知道，西湖的风景非常美丽。

Exercise

从下面四个选项中选出最佳答案。

1. _____, this decision is totally reasonable.

   A. I hope   B. Considering   C. In my opinion   D.Talking of

2. _____, you have little chance of passing the exam.

   A. I hope   B. To be honest   C. Talking of   D. I know

3. For that matter, _____, she made a firm decision.

   A. however   B. true   C. wonderful   D. besides

4. _____, the police caught the prisoner.

   A. Fortunately   B. Although   C. Otherwise   D. So as

参考答案：

1. C   2. B   3. A   4. A

第二单元　倒装句 1：部分倒装

部分倒装：将谓语的一部分放在主语的前面，比如助动词或情态动词。

比较：
主语在前，谓语在后 → 自然语序
主语在后，谓语在前 → 倒装语序

1 在含有 Not only ... but also ...（不仅……而且……）的句子中，not only 之后的句子要部分倒装，而 but also 之后的句子不倒装。

> not only 后的句子把 does 放在主语 my brother 前面，构成部分倒装

· Not only **does my brother** like swimming, but also he likes playing basketball.

> but also 后的句子不倒装

我哥哥不仅喜欢游泳，而且也喜欢打篮球。

2 在 "only + 状语 / 状语从句" 置于句首的情况下，主句要部分倒装。

> can 放在主语 I 前面，构成部分倒装

· Only in this way **can I** pass the final exam.

只有这样我才能通过期末考试。

3 not until 出现在句首时，用于引导主从复合句，主句要倒装，从句不倒装，表示"直到……才……"。这时主句和从句中间不需用逗号隔开。如果 not until 没有位于句首，就不需要倒装。

> 从句不倒装

· Not until I told him **did he** know the truth.

> 主句把 did 放在主语 he 的前面，构成部分倒装

直到我告诉他，他才知道真相。

> not until 没有位于句首，不需要倒装

· It was not until I told him that **he knew** the truth.

直到我告诉他，他才知道真相。

4 句首出现 sometimes，usually，often，always，almost never，many a time 等表示频率的副词或副词短语时，句子要部分倒装。

> does 放在主语 my mother 前面，构成部分倒装

· Sometimes **does my mother** go to work by bus.

我妈妈有时坐公交车去上班。

5 含有 were，should，had 的虚拟条件句中，通常可以省略引导词 if，此时要部分倒装，将 were，had，should 移到主语的前面。

= Were I you

• If I were you, I wouldn't waste the precious time.

如果我是你，我就不会浪费宝贵的时间。

= Had you

• If you had listened to your parents, your life would be better.

如果你听了你父母的话，你的生活会更好。

= Should it

• If it should rain tomorrow, they will not go outside.

明天要是下雨的话，他们就不出去了。

6 句首出现 never，hardly，seldom，nowhere，scarcely，by no means，no sooner 等否定词或否定词组，主句要部分倒装。

had 放在主语 we 的前面，构成部分倒装

• Hardly had we lain down when the doorbell rang.

我们刚一躺下，门铃就响了。

have 放在主语 I 的前面，构成部分倒装

• Never have I met such a generous man.

我从未见过这么大方的人。

does 放在主语 he 的前面，构成部分倒装

• Seldom does he drink cola.

他很少喝可乐。

7 as 或 though 引导的让步状语从句，从句使用部分倒装，其结构是：形容词 / 副词 / 名词 + as/though + 主语 + 谓语。

把形容词放在 as/though 的前面

• Poor as/though the man is, he is still willing to help others.

虽然这个人很穷，但他仍然愿意帮助别人。

8 如果前面的肯定情况也适用于后者，可以用"so + be 动词 / 助动词 / 情态动词 + 主语"倒装结构。

用于表示我也喜欢唱歌

• Tina likes singing. So do I.

蒂娜喜欢唱歌。我也一样。

常用"so + 主语 + be 动词 / 助动词 / 情态动词"结构表达"是这样，的确如此"的含义。

— Your father is a lawyer.
你爸爸是一名律师。
— So he is.
他的确是。

9 如果前面的否定情况也适用于后者，可以用"neither/nor + be 动词 / 助动词 / 情态动词 + 主语"倒装结构。

• Jerry isn't good at swimming. Neither/Nor am I.

用于表示我也不擅长游泳

杰瑞不擅长游泳，我也不擅长。

第三单元 倒装句 2：完全倒装

完全倒装：将谓语部分全部放在主语前面。

1 There be 句型引起的完全倒装。

把 are 放在主语 students 的前面

- **There are** ten students in the classroom.

教室里有十名学生。

2 句首出现表示地点、时间、方向的副词时，一般要用完全倒装结构。如果主语是代词，则不需要用倒装结构。

主语是代词，不用倒装

- **Here it** is.

在这里。

把 comes 放在主语 the bus 的前面

- **Here comes** the bus.

公交车来了。

3 句首出现表示地点的介词短语，且其后接 be 动词或 come，lie，live，exist，stand，sit 等时，通常要用完全倒装。

in front of 表示地点，其后用完全倒装

- **In front of** my house **lies** a fruit tree.

我的房子前面有一棵果树。

4 如果 so 修饰的形容词或副词位于句首，其后的句子要用完全倒装。

完全倒装

- **So kind** is the woman that she was deceived.

这个女人太善良了，她被欺骗了。

5 表语置于句首，会引起完全倒装。

useful 放在句首，完全倒装

- **Useful is** the information.

这个信息很有用。

nice 放在句首，完全倒装

- **Nice looks** this furniture.

这件家具看起来不错。

Exercise

一、判断下面句子是正常语序还是倒装语序。

1. She is not only a writer but also a singer. (　　)

2. Not only is she a writer but also a singer. (　　)

3. Had I time, I would have prepared well for the exam. (　　)

4. If I had time, I would have prepared well for the exam. (　　)

5. I didn't realize it until the teacher pointed out my mistake. (　　)

6. Not until the teacher pointed out my mistake did I realize it. (　　)

二、将下列单词按照正确的顺序排序，使用倒装语序。

1. are many books on there desk the

_____

2. books are here your

_____

3. fine I would go should it to park the be

_____

4. a man lies balcony the on

_____

5. was did she realize she then only wrong that

_____

参考答案：
一、1. 正常语序　2. 倒装语序　3. 倒装语序　4. 正常语序　5. 正常语序　6. 倒装语序
二、1. There are many books on the desk.
　　2. Here are your books.
　　3. Should it be fine, I would go to the park.
　　4. On the balcony lies a man.
　　5. Only then did she realize that she was wrong.

第四单元 强调句

强调句常用来强调主语、宾语、状语等句子成分，也可以用来加强语气或表达某种意愿、情感等。

强调句的结构

1 强调句的结构是"**It is/was + 被强调部分 + that/who + 其他成分**"。被强调部分指人的时候关系代词就用 **that/who**，指物的时候就用 **that**。

强调的是 Linda，关系代词可以用 that 或 who

· It was **Linda that/who** helped us in trouble.

是琳达在困境中帮助了我们。

强调的是 blackboard，关系代词用 that

· It was **the blackboard that** the student broke yesterday.

这个学生昨天打破的是黑板。

在强调句中，即使被强调的主语是复数，主句中的谓语动词依然用单数。

2 被强调部分是时间、地点、方式、原因状语时，连接从句的关系词也只能用 **that**。

强调的是时间，关系代词也只能用 that

· It was **yesterday that** I lost my wallet.

我是昨天丢的钱包。

强调的是地点，关系代词也只能用 that

· It was **the store that** my mother went to.

我妈妈去的是那家商店。

表示强调的其他结构

1 用 **very，single，only，such，last** 等形容词来修饰名词或形容词，可表示强调。

用 last 修饰 one 表示强调

· I am the **last one** that come to the classroom.

我是最后一个到教室的人。

2 用助动词 **do/does/did** 表示强调。

助动词 do 表示强调

· **Do** lock the door before you leave.

离开前一定要锁门。

3 可以反复使用同一个单词（动词、副词、形容词、名词等）来表示强调。

反复使用 hours 来表示强调

· He plays computer games for **hours and hours**.

他玩电脑游戏好几个小时了。

4 反身代词也可以表示强调。

反身代词 yourself 表示强调

· You should wash the clothes **yourself**.

你应该自己洗衣服。

5 某些介词短语可用于疑问句中加强语气：**on earth，at all，in the world**。

on earth 表示强调

· What **on earth** do you want?

你究竟想要什么？

Exercise

一、找出下列句子的错误之处并改正。

1. It was the park where I went for a walk in the evening. _____

2. It was in the evening when I went for a walk in the park. _____

3. What in world do you want to do? _____

4. It were my mother who bought me the books. _____

5. It is the new dress who is my present. _____

二、圈出下列句子中表示强调的部分。

1. This is the very book I'm looking for. 这正是我要找的那本书。

2. You can fulfill the task yourself. 你可以自己完成这个任务。

3. It was Lily who taught me to paint. 是莉莉教我画画的。

4. Do be quiet. The class begins. 保持安静，要上课了。

5. Do you know at all? 你究竟知不知道？

6. It was Tina that hit the table. 撞桌子的是蒂娜。

7. It is they that are going to the beach. 是他们要去海边。

8. It was ants that destroyed the dam. 是蚂蚁摧毁了大坝。

9. What in the world happened there? 那里到底发生了什么？

10. It was Bell that invented the telephone. 是贝尔发明了电话。

参考答案：
一、1. where → that　2. when → that　3. in world → in the world
　4. were → was　5. who → that
二、1. the very book　2. yourself　3. Lily　4. Do　5. at all
　6. Tina　7. they　8. ants　9. in the world　10. Bell

第五单元 直接引语和间接引语

直接引语：直接引用别人的原话，两边用引号标出。

间接引语：用自己的语言转述别人的话，不需要引号。

转换为间接引语时，句子的结构、人称、时态、时间状语和地点状语等都要有变化。

1 人称的转变

⊙ 直接引语中的第一人称 → 第三人称

· She said, "I am very sorry."

→ She said that she was very sorry.

⊙ 直接引语中的第二人称，如果原话是针对转述人说的 → 第一人称。

· My teacher told me, "You should study harder."

→ My teacher told me that I should study harder.

⊙ 直接引语中的第二人称，如果原话是针对第三人称说的 → 第三人称

· She said to her son, "I will buy some fruit for you."

→ She said to her son that she would buy some fruit for him.

· The girl said to her friend, "I'll come to your house."

→ The girl said to her friend that she would come to her house.

2 时态的转换

直接引语改为间接引语时，主句中的谓语动词如果是过去时，从句（即间接引语部分）的谓语动词在时态方面要作相应的变化，变成过去时范畴的各种时态（实际也是宾语从句的时态要求）。

直接引语	间接引语
一般现在时	一般过去时
现在进行时	过去进行时
现在完成时	过去完成时
一般过去时	过去完成时
过去进行时	过去进行时（不变）
过去完成时	过去完成时（不变）
一般将来时	过去将来时

· "I am going to visit you." she said.

→ She said she was going to visit us.

· Tom asked, "Have you closed the door before you left?"

→ Tom asked me whether I had closed the door before I left.

· Linda said, "We are enjoying the play."

→ Linda said they were enjoying the play.

3 直接引语变成间接引语时，从句时态无须改变的情况：

◎ 当主句的谓语动词是一般现在时的时候。

- He always **says**, "I **have tried** my best."

  → He always says that he **has tried** his best.

◎ 当主句的谓语动词是将来时的时候。

- She **will say**, "**I will** try my best to realise the goal."

  → She will say that she **will try** her best to realise the goal.

◎ 当直接引语中有情态动词时。

- The doctor said, "You **should** take medicine after meals."

  → The doctor said I **should** take medicine after meals.

◎ 当直接引语部分带有具体的过去时间状语时。

- She said, "I **graduated in 2012**."

  → She told us that she **graduated in 2012**.

◎ 当直接引语中有以 **when**，**while** 引导的从句，表示过去的时间时。

- He said, "**When** I was a child, I usually **played** basketball with my father."

  → He said that when he was a child, he usually **played** basketball with his father.

◎ 当直接引语是客观真理、自然现象、谚语时。

- Our teacher said to us, "The moonlight we saw **comes** from the sun."

  → Our teacher told us that the moonlight we saw **comes** from the sun.

4 时间状语、地点状语及某些对比性的指示代词和动词变化：

	直接引语	间接引语
指示代词	this/these	that/those
	now	then
	today	that day
	tonight	that night
	this week/month ...	that week/month ...
时间状语	yesterday	the day before
	last week/month ...	the week/month ... before
	two weeks/months ago	two weeks/months before
	tomorrow	the next day
	next week/month ...	the next week/month ...
地点状语	here	there
动词	come	go
	bring	take

第六单元 There be 句型

There be 句型

◉ 肯定句：
- **There is** a flower pot on the table.
  桌子上有一个花盆。
- **There were** many people in the hall yesterday.
  昨天大厅里有很多人。

◉ 否定句：
- There is **not any** water in the glass.
  = There is **no** water in the glass.
  玻璃杯里没有水了。

◉ 一般疑问句：
- **Is there** a cat in the yard?
  院子里有只猫吗？
- **Are there** any books on the desk?
  桌子上有书吗？

There be 句型和 have 的区别

There be 句型表示"某地有某人"或"某地有某物"，而 **have** 表示"主语拥有某人或某物"。

there are 表示房间里有床
- **There are** two beds in the room.
  房间里有两张床。

have 表示我有家庭作业
- I **have** too much homework to do.
  我有太多的家庭作业要做。

There be 句型的知识补充

1 **There is no use (in) doing sth** 表示"做……没用"，其中 **in** 可以省略，相当于 "**It is no use doing sth**"。
- There is no use (in) reasoning with her.
  = It is no use reasoning with her.
  和她讲道理是没有用的。

2 **There be (not) + 名词 + to do/to be done** 表示"（没）有……要做"。
- There is much housework to do.
  = There is much housework to be done.
  还有很多家务活要做。

3 情态动词 **used to，have to，ought to** 可用于 **There be** 句型中。
- There ought to be another chance to win.
  应该还有一次获胜的机会。

4 **There is a possibility ...** 表示"有可能……"。
- There is a possibility that we may give up this plan.
  我们有可能会放弃这个计划。

5 **There be certain/sure to be ...** 表示"肯定有……"。
- There are certain/sure to be some merits in this plan.
  这个计划肯定有一些优点。

Exercise

一、在空格处填上合适的 be 动词，补全句子。

1. There _____ an umbrella behind the door.

2. There _____ many books on the shelf.

3. There _____ hardly any smell in the refrigerator.

4. There _____ two dogs in the garden.

5. There _____ two chairs in the living room.

6. There _____ a few people on the playground.

二、从下面四个选项中选出最佳答案。

1. There _____ three pictures on the wall.

    A. is   B. was   C. are   D. be

2. There is no use _____ regretting now.

    A. in   B. on   C. at   D. to

3. There are still many clothes _____.

    A. wash   B. to wash   C. washing   D. washed

4. There is _____ possibility that situation will get worse.

    A. a   B. an   C. /   D. the

参考答案：

一、1. is 2. are 3. is 4. are 5. are 6. are

二、1. C 2. A 3. B 4. A